"I have read *Decide to Survive* and I have traveled much of Brittany's journey with her. I am her mother, her friend, and her cheerleader! Brittany made a choice to make a change in her life—it wasn't easy, and it didn't happen over overnight, but she did it and continues to do it! I believe this book can help others find their worth in themselves and find the people in their lives who will help them start that change!"

Jackie Rathjen, Brittany's Mother

"Brittany's story is that of empowerment and resilience! She is living proof that it takes work, perseverance and strength to face difficult life challenges. Her 'can do' attitude is contagious, and *Decide to Survive* is potentially a motivator for anyone struggling with mental illness, substance abuse, domestic violence or sexual abuse."

Christy Buck, Executive Director Mental Health Foundation and Founder of be nice. Co-author of *be nice. Four Simple Steps to Recognize Depression & Prevent Suicide*

"Many of our families have a story similar to Brittany's story, *Decide to Survive*. Unfortunately, most of us live in communities where shame has stigmatized the events that have hurt the most. This honest and insightful story of raw truth and recovery can be used to open dialogue and begin the healing process no matter who we are or where we live. Read it. Use it to heal. Let it become a template for you to tell your own story of hope and healing."

Jim Liske, Pastor & Leader Development; former Prison Fellowship President & CEO

"Brittany's success over addiction shows that addiction can be 'cured'—It can fix the 'hole in your soul' and address the 'why' of your addiction, just as Brittany did. And, it does not have to be a 'hopeless, one day at a time' approach. Congratulations, Brittany. *Decide to Survive* is an inspiration."

Jane Patterson, Ottawa County,
Michigan Mental Health Court Representative

"*Decide to Survive* is as compelling as any Hollywood drama I've ever seen or read. It is remarkable and, quite frankly, a miracle that she bounced back from so many brushes against death and disaster and managed to come back in one piece. In some ways, it seems like an impossible achievement, but the main takeaway this story provides is that anyone who wants to escape whatever living hell they find themselves in, can come back and live a happy, healthy, productive life."

Chip Brown, President & CEO, Storyastic

"*Decide to Survive* shows her determination to change her life as she boldly, honestly shares her bout with hell and offers practical help to create hope for others."

Kim Advent, Professional Wellness Educator

"Brittany's life story is one of hope for those who suffer from addiction and mental health struggles. From darkness came inspiration. I'm honored to know her and her story."

Joe Slenk, Police Officer, friend and supporter of Brittany

Decide to Survive

How I Beat Addiction (& How You Can Too)

Thank you so much
For your Support
God Bless
you & the
Family
xoxo

Decide to Survive

How I Beat Addiction (& How You Can Too)

By Brittany Midolo

propermedia

WE Be Nice, LLC 159 S. River Avenue Unit 505, Holland, Mi. 49423

Disclaimer:
The **be nice.** action plan and its steps to notice, invite, challenge, and empower
are effective steps to helping yourself or someone who is experiencing a mental
health concern or crisis. This action plan is by no means a replacement for
appropriate medical care or professional help. This tool is to be used as a means
to aid in the process of bettering an individual's mental health or decreasing a
person's risk for suicide. This book is not a tool to diagnose yourself or someone
with a mental illness. When used appropriately this tool has been proven to
reduce behavioral referrals and increase a person's likelihood to seek help
concerning their mental health. It is also proven to aid as a positive culture
shift when it comes to mental health and the way we treat others.

Mention of specific companies, organizations, or authorities in this book does
not imply endorsement by the author or publisher, nor does mention of specific
companies, organizations, or authorities imply they endorse this book, its author,
or publisher.

John Corriveau - photograph of authors
Chip Brown - Proper Media for editorial, design and supply chain
Chris Tiegreen - editorial
First edition: 2023 10 9 8 7 6 5 4 3 2
Printed in the United States of America.
Ordering information: jeff@elhart.com www.WEbenice.org

For my family, and everyone struggling through life facing dark times due to addiction and mental health, looking for new beginning and healthier times. I am sharing my story of hope with you, so you may find your path to happiness as well.

Contents

Foreword

I knew Brittany's grandparents, in fact we were neighbors. I didn't know Brittany until one day she called me in desperation looking for help. Because of my admiration for her parents, I listened. I listened because of my personal experience of living through family trauma of the loss of my brother from depression and by suicide. From that personal experience, I became an advocate for suicide prevention education on a national, state and local level. Brittany's voice sounded like many others of which I have literally spoken to hundreds since my brother's death with desperation in their voice either for a concern of themselves or a concern for a loved one's well-being.

My hope is you are not personally experiencing the trauma of the many experiences that Brittany has had in her life like mental illness, substance abuse, sexual abuse, homelessness among others, but you are concerned about someone you love who may be experiencing trauma in their lives. These traumatic experiences can be hidden or they can be visually very apparent. Regardless, people ridden with the grasp of addiction and abuse often go unnoticed as their experience can be embarrassing and helplessness takes over in their mind. I know it did in my brother's case of depression.

Brittany's life experiences have involved what I call the four pillars to high suicide risk. Mental illness, substance abuse, sexual abuse and domestic violence are experiences that dramatically increase the likelihood of suicide. Here is the problem and the answer. These four experiences are treatable. Suicide is preventable. How? By being equipped with the ability to notice what is right about someone and then notice the changes in their behavior. Next, by inviting yourself to have a caring conversation about what you have noticed in their change in behavior provides the person that someone actually cares, and the journey that they have been on is not forsaken. Then, by challenging the person with your love with tough questions can open up opportunities for you to earn their trust to take the final step to empower yourself to get them the professional treatment that they need to survive. These are the steps you will be left with after reading Brittany's journey through Hell. Brittany uses these steps now by helping others before they fall off the deep end.

The story of Brittany unfolds her life as a sweet girl raised by a loving family to the dark stage of her life that left her homeless and with more trauma that one can imagine. As you read through Brittany's roller coaster of ups and downs, you'll ask yourself, "How can she make it out of this dark and deep hole alive?" This is the powerful obstacle that Brittany proclaims as her greatest success in life. In her words, "I got this!" and her decision to "decide to survive" should resonate with you as a motivator, as she beat addiction and you can too.

I am proud to call Brittany my friend. She encourages me to continue my own journey as a suicide prevention education advocate. Many people in her situation may not have made it through the other side as she did. Brittany's book is a second in my dream to equip people to become lifeguards rather than bystanders for loved ones suffering with mental illness, addiction, sexual abuse and domestic violence. My first book, **be nice. – 4 SIMPLE STEPS To Recognize Depression and Prevent Suicide** provides readers the "Stop, Drop and Roll" of helping a friend or loved one with depression before it's too late as it was for my brother. I am proud to publish this work of Brittany's and look forward to the many lives she will help through her shared experiences.

—Jeff Elhart

Preface

"I need to raise $300,000 to stay here, or I'm going to be sent home," said the voice on the phone.

"Who is this again?" I asked.

"Brittany. You remember Dick Rademaker's granddaughter?"

"Oh sure, I remember you, Brittany. Now, what are you asking me about? $300,000 for what?"

"Well, I'm here in Argentina at a drug rehabilitation center. I've been here for about a year now, and it costs a lot of money to stay. If I don't have the money, I'll have to leave and won't be able to complete my treatment. I don't want to go back to the life I lived as an addict."

"Wow. Can you explain the program you're in? I can't fathom how or why it's so expensive."

For the next hour, Brittany told me about her treatment. I still couldn't quite comprehend what I was hearing. Thirty thousand dollars a month for treatment! But their success rate of treating drug addicts was nearly 100 percent. My perception of drug addicts was that most remained stuck in their lifestyle of stealing, lying, and manipulating and never found their way out. A near 100-percent success rate is incredible.

After a couple of phone conversations with Brittany and her coach, I realized how brave she was to call and ask for money to save her life. I decided it was worth listening to her—and maybe even helping her out financially.

Within the next sixty days, I found myself hosting a fundraiser: "Saving Brittany." I and about thirty people at my business watched and listened as she told the story of her journey with drugs. She shared her treatment experience with us and said she was doing really well. She no longer had any interest in drugs. The urge was gone.

We listened to her philosophy coaches and the stories of how well Brittany was doing in her rehabilitation. The photos from when she first entered the treatment center painted a dramatic picture of physical transformation and proved how serious she was taking her rehab. This desperate young woman's story pulled at our heartstrings and convinced me and many other community members to come to her rescue by helping her continue and ultimately complete her lifesaving treatment.

Decide to Survive is a heart-wrenching, inspirational, and gratifying story. Brittany's decision to survive and thrive from the dirty world of drug addiction will encourage and empower you and your loved ones to decide to survive as well. Her personal journey and how it impacted her family and friends could have ended like many others—in a deadly overdose. But, with the help of others, she convinced herself that she could change the direction of her life.

Many who battle addiction, as well those who care for them, will see hope in this story of never giving up. Instead of feeling there's no way out, they may even find themselves thinking what Brittany so often says: "I got this," and they will likely decide to survive—and thrive—themselves.

—Jeff Elhart

Introduction

"You'll be fine," the attorney said.

He was court-appointed to my case on the spot, and I'd talked with him for all of two minutes before I had to go before the judge. But he was sure, after I'd been clean for two-and-a-half years, that this was just a matter of procedure. The judge would quickly give me probation, I'd serve it out, and I could put my past behind me forever.

That was a comforting thought, but my heart was still pounding, especially as I looked at all the guys in chains around me waiting their turn. I thought I had left that world, and now I felt like I was being put right back into the middle of it. One by one, the guys in chains were called before the judge, and my name was about to come up.

In spite of the lawyer's assurances, I was still terrified.

I got up to the stand and was talking with the judge about the charges against me: possession of all the drugs that were in the house when my husband died. Suddenly, a voice from the other side of the room interrupted us. "We also want to charge her with cause of death," he said.

My heart sank, I turned pale, and I could hear my mother start to cry.

The lawyers went up to the bench to talk, and it seemed like they were there forever, even though it wasn't that long. I was so nervous as I watched them walk back. I did not want to go back to that life. I knew that if I had to go to prison, I'd come out as that rough, gruff person again.

I just didn't know if I had it in me.

The story of how I got to that pivotal moment is a painful one, and I don't remember all the details. Drugs have a way of affecting memories, and I have tried not to dwell on the memories anyway. And the story of how I got through those times and put them behind me isn't typical. Most people with a heroin addiction end up either dead or in prison. Statistically, I'm a rare exception.

But these are important stories to tell because a lot of people and their families face the challenges of an addiction, and I don't have to be an exception.

This is not a story that starts on the streets, in a crisis, or in a disadvantaged situation. We were a middle-class family in a good community. We faced typical challenges and handled them like most families do until a sequence of events and decisions led to a nightmare for all of us.

I am writing this book because we came out of that nightmare. It took a lot of love and sacrifice, and at times it looked impossible, but I am a testimony that nothing is impossible. For anyone who has experienced addiction, knows someone who has, or simply wants to help with one of today's most destructive social problems, there is hope.

There is always hope.

My Normal Life

I don't remember much from when I was young. In many ways, it was a normal childhood. My family did the kinds of things most families did—we took vacations together, went to church on Sundays, and had a home life that most people would think of as ordinary. My parents tell me I was precocious, full of personality, always into something, full-steam-ahead right from the start. Everything seemed to be fine. I was just a kid who enjoyed life.

My life began in Chicago, where I was born ten months after my parents were told it might take a long time for them to have children. I came a little earlier than expected too, so they weren't quite ready for me. My father and grandmother painted my room while my mom was still in the hospital, and they say the paint didn't even have time to dry before I came home. My family called me Boo Bear because my eyes were so big that it looked like someone had scared me. They made up a song about Boo Bear and sang it to me often. My grandfather called me that a lot, and the name means the world to me. Every time I hear it, I think of my Pops and know he's still with me.

My parents moved to Kalamazoo to go to Western Michigan University when I was about four months old. We lived in "married housing," and because both of them were in school—my dad was studying to be a police officer and my mom was studying to be a special ed teacher—we didn't have much money at all. My dad had big dreams and worked hard at a pizza place to make sure we all had what we needed. I think we must have lived off of mac and cheese and pizza while they were in school. They struggled like many young married couples do, but they both worked very hard for everything we had.

I'm told I had a best friend named Johnny and that he and I would get into everything. I don't remember that because I was so young, but I love hearing my parents' stories about it. Johnny and I went outside and played in the mud one morning before church, and apparently that kind of thing wasn't unusual for us. My parents had to put locks all the way at the top of the door because I knew how to push chairs over to it and get us out of the room. But I was a handful on my own too. I didn't sleep well at night—the police once came to check on us because I yelled out the window, "I will be good!" and someone thought I was being hurt. I was very vocal and very active, always on the go.

After my parents graduated, my father got a job as a police officer in Battle Creek and my mother got a job teaching special needs kids at a public school. I liked her job. She taught my brother and me sign language, and she helped a lot of kids in difficult situations. Some of her students were beaten at home, and the only place they could get away was at school. Both of my parents were in jobs that helped people with their problems.

I was a normal girl with a normal upbringing and the kinds of struggles that most kids have. My younger brother came along when I was 4, and I liked carrying him and playing with him. His name was Johnny too. My parents told me I used to go get him up from his nap, and sometimes they would hear him fall out of his crib and then my voice saying, "Oops, dropped the baby!" That seemed to happen a lot.

When we got older, we pushed the limits sometimes. One day my parents went for a walk, and when they came back, I had cut a bunch of bald spots into Johnny's hair. But he and I have always gotten along, even from the beginning. I loved being an older sister.

I had a lot of self-esteem as a child. My parents describe me as feisty, fun-loving, and very independent. They would try to teach me things like how to brush my teeth or tie my shoes, and I'd tell them I knew how—even when I didn't—and try to do it myself. Even as I grew older, I would always tell them, "I've got this." I liked to have my routine and do things my way. It was always an intentional, strong conviction to decide to thrive. I was a good swimmer and even set some records for my age when we lived in Battle Creek. I was especially good at the breaststroke and loved being in the water. My parents told me I was like a fish. Swimming was one of several things in life that gave me a lot of confidence in myself.

When I was around 10, my parents decided to move to Zeeland, Michigan, to work for my grandfather's company. I don't think that was an easy move for me, and I didn't want to go at first. Our new home was okay, but it was hard to leave my friends behind. But I got used to it, and eventually I loved it. I didn't continue swimming after we moved, which my parents still regret and wish they had pushed me to keep it up. But for whatever reason, I decided I didn't want to do it anymore.

I made friends in Zeeland, and being with my grandparents was good for me. I've always had a good relationship with my grandparents on both sides of the family. Pops and Gerks were my mother's parents in Zeeland, and I grew really close to them after we moved there. Pops was very funny and always had a smile on his face. Gerks was very spirited, always willing to say what was on her mind, no matter what it was—just very honest and true. She was always there for me, just a phone call away, and I called her often to get her opinion on things going on in my life. I felt only acceptance and never any judgment from either of them. They cared a lot, and they were fun to be around.

I loved going over to their house. Pops became like a father figure to me. We went everywhere together. He taught me everything I needed to know about cooking. He took me out on his boat often, and he would always buy me candy. Sometimes we had movie nights at my grandparents' house, and I would stay overnight with them. I remember one time when Pops bought a motor scooter, and Gerks wanted to try it out. She ended up running it into a wall, but she was adventurous like that. She wanted to give things a try, and it made their home a fun atmosphere. When I stayed with them, I'd help with chores, give them backrubs, and help cook. Pops was full of jokes and made up songs all the time, and he enjoyed waking up my grandmother and me by banging pots and pans and yelling silly rhymes. Their home was a happy place.

I remember thinking, even when I was very young, that I wanted to be like them. I could tell that they were in love, and I always wanted a relationship like the one they had. They seemed to understand me even when I didn't understand myself, and they were always available to me. I really learned a lot from them. They had so much love and cared so much about each other and other people. It was amazing to see.

I was also close to my dad's parents: GG and Grandpa (his mom and stepdad) and Papa and Nana (his dad and stepmom). It wasn't quite as easy to visit them, since they were all in Chicago, but I still saw them often and enjoyed staying with them. To this day, GG and I are very close. She's 4'8" with glasses and a bowl haircut, always sewing and making things. She used to take my brother and me on shopping trips, and we'd load up on whatever we wanted. I remember crawling in bed with her when I was little to wake her up in the morning. We'd play "beauty"—I'd do her nails and her hair—or we'd make things together. She was always available for me, and even now I call her with every little thing. We're always on the phone together, and my husband and I try to visit her at least once a month.

Papa and Nana lived in Florida for part of the year, and I remember visiting them there sometimes too. But I saw them more often when they were in their home in Chicago. They had a game room where we hung out and played pool, and I got to spend time with them sometimes when they came to see my brother's hockey games. Nana loved roller coasters, so when we went to Wisconsin Dells, an amusement park, she went on all the rides with us. They were always on the go and full of life.

I also have two aunts I loved hanging out with. Jodi, my mom's sister, was really close by. She lived on a blueberry farm at one point, and we used to go there and pick blueberries. She was a great cook too—she owned a restaurant and catering service in Holland where I worked for a couple of years in high school—and we'd always make pizzas together when we visited. She would take us on what we call "Jodi adventures." I had a great time with her, and with Ashley, my dad's sister. She's super-funny, and I have always been able to joke around with her. I loved going to stay with her in Chicago too. I grew up in a great, supportive family.

Zeeland is an amazing community—family-oriented, supportive, conservative, with a very strong religious background. Like a lot of people, our family went to church regularly, and I remember the community as a loving environment. It has changed a lot over the years, but many of those characteristics are still there.

There were always opportunities to help others in Zeeland—it was that kind of community—and through our church, our family also went on several mission trips to Jamaica. We worked in the mountains and helped build houses for people on one trip, and even though it was hard work, I remember it as a really fun time. We played games together, put up with a lot of beetles, and drew close as a family. I also went on other trips to Montego Bay in Jamaica, once with my family and once with our church youth group, and helped with children in orphanages, playing with them, feeding them, painting with them, and teaching them. I learned a lot of sign language on one of those trips too. I felt very involved and benefitted very much from growing up in a community where values like these were common.

But there's another side to that experience too. A lot of expectations come with those values. I felt a lot of support, but I also felt a lot of pressure to be perfect. It's a small town, and things get around. Mistakes like speeding tickets get published in the newspaper. I didn't feel like I lived up to everyone's expectations, and I think some of my later rebellion came because of that pressure. No matter how much support you have from the people around you, it still isn't easy when you feel like you're always falling short.

But it wasn't just the community or my family. I put a lot of pressure on myself too. About the time I was in junior high, I started to hate myself, although it may have started even earlier than that. I can't remember exactly when and why those feelings first started, but my mom says it became clear as I struggled in junior high to make good grades. I didn't think I was smart enough and started to see myself as dumb. I really didn't like myself or view myself very highly, I was frustrated that I didn't do well in school, and it was easier after a while not to even try. Over time, all the self-esteem I had as a little girl seemed to disappear. In fact, I remember at one point in junior high thinking I really didn't like anything about myself. Maybe I was trying too hard to please my parents, or maybe I just felt like I needed to be number one at everything and never reached that goal. I felt like I was letting everyone down. Keeping up with people's expectations, or even my own, began to feel like a losing battle. But it's still hard for me to know exactly how and why it all started.

Junior high generally was not a good time for me. I had trouble learning because of ADHD and dyslexia, which, of course, only fed those negative feelings. I probably didn't care about how well I did in school when I was younger, but academic aptitude becomes a little more obvious as you get older, and I could tell I wasn't keeping up with other classmates. Even though I'd grown up with a lot of confidence, I started to feel like I didn't know how to do anything well. Not doing well at school became part of my identity, something I would just have to accept about myself.

And my learning disabilities were not only hard on me; they were hard on the whole family. Academics had always come so easily for my father, so he never understood the difficulties I was having. Maybe that's one reason I turned to my grandfather so much. He and my mother, who has always been like a friend to me, gave me a lot of support, but it was still a difficult time.

My father had a great relationship with my brother. Absolutely flawless. Both of them loved hockey. My dad had played hockey when he was younger and was really good at it, and Johnny became a really good player too. He probably could have gone pro later if not for having too many concussions. So when he was playing on teams as a kid, dad would go to all his games, and they traveled together often. They bonded over hockey and always got along.

Johnny was good at everything. He and I have always been very close, but we are very different. I was a handful, and he was always easy for my parents. He was great at school and seemed to do all the right things. He was my dad's pride and joy, and I knew I wasn't as good as him in anything. Even though I loved my brother and we shared some of the same friends, I felt less-than. He was on track in life, and I knew I wasn't.

My feelings about myself weren't just about classes and grades. I began to hate the way I looked during junior high. I never thought I was pretty enough or skinny enough. I felt very isolated and alone.

I didn't feel like anyone really understood how much I didn't like myself, and how some of their actions made that worse. I didn't understand why things came so easily for other people but not for me. I felt like I was never enough—that no matter what I did, it was never going to be enough for anyone. In reality, it wasn't enough for me. And I felt very empty inside.

Do You Need Immediate Help?

For Immediate help,
call the 988 Suicide and Crisis Lifeline,
available 24/7.
https://988lifeline.org/media-resources/
"If you or someone you know is experiencing a mental health or substance use crisis, call or text 988"

When Things Began to Change

We had a pretty normal life, and of course it was normal to me because it's all I knew. And anyone looking in from the outside would have called us a typical family too. I had parents who worked hard at good jobs and a brother who was a superstar hockey player, and we all did things together. We had some great vacations, went to hockey games, and had a family game night. I was involved in things at school, played a few sports and danced, and knew there were people in my life who were on my side. Sure, I had some struggles, and my parents didn't always approve of my friends, but these are typical teenage problems.

But even though I really had little to complain about, I hated myself more and more. And as far as I knew, that's what normal looked like.

I was still as much of a fireball as I had been when I was little, so I got detention a lot—"Saturday school." It didn't help that I started hanging out with the wrong people. I got suspended once because I thought a teacher was racist and spit on his door. I don't know why I thought that. At the time, I was with a friend who didn't like him very much, and she was Hispanic and may have thought he had some prejudices, so maybe I was just picking up on her attitude and sticking up for her. I always tended to speak up for people who I felt might need someone to defend them—a good quality to have, but one that may have gotten me into a lot of trouble at times. In any case, my mom says he was one of the nicest teachers I ever had and was just trying to help me out. (He's actually my next-door neighbor today—and definitely not a racist.) But since I wasn't passing any classes and didn't want to be there anyway, I just kind of followed my friend and didn't mind stirring up trouble.

Sometimes I got in trouble just because of who I was hanging out with. Some of my friends decided that putting marijuana inside of Sharpie pens was a great way to distribute it to students who wanted it without getting caught. But they did get caught, and because they were my friends, I was searched to make sure I didn't have any pot on me. I didn't, but I think teachers assumed I was at least somewhat guilty because I was good friends with those who were actually guilty. It definitely didn't help my reputation.

I got a lot of detentions because of one teacher who talked and acted like a male chauvinist. I told him what I thought of him often, and every time he would assign me to Saturday school for talking back. He really did seem to have some attitude problems with female students (and their mothers), but somehow I never learned just to keep my mouth shut. I talked back to other teachers too—sometimes for protesting tests that I thought weren't fair, sometimes for speaking up for people who needed help, and sometimes just because I felt like making trouble. Whatever the reason, I was in Saturday school more often than not.

My parents remember getting phone calls from the school all the time, especially during the last three weeks of junior high, when I essentially spent the entire time with the vice principal. They got to know the school administrators very well. They joked with my brother that he would have to be good because I used up all the detentions. But even though they were concerned, they didn't consider my naughtiness to be anything other than that—just a young teenager trying to figure out her niche while struggling academically and hanging out with the wrong crowd. A lot of people would consider these typical kinds of problems, and as far as they knew, that's all that was going on.

But there were signs of deeper issues. Once when we were having a "family night"—we used to love watching *Survivor* together—I got angry about something that no one remembers and went downstairs to my bedroom. I kept yelling at my parents and slamming the door to show how angry I was. My dad came downstairs and took the door of the hinges. A little while later, they heard me hammering as I nailed a blanket to the door frame.

Maybe that's why some of my family called me manic. I didn't have much control of my feelings during this time. I'd go from super-happy to extremely frustrated, and no one really knew why. One minute I'd be laughing with them, and the next I'd be arguing with them. I remember laughing really hard and then hearing someone say something that instantly filled me with anger, or I'd be sad and then would start laughing without having a good reason for it. I was very up and down. Sometimes people would tell me I had everything I wanted or needed and ask me how I could be this way, and I never knew what to say. My moods went up and down for no apparent reason.

Some teachers noticed my mood swings and would try to help. One put a lot of time and effort into helping me make it through junior high, even to the point of having me over to eat dinner with her family. There were a few activities I thought I was good at—I loved to dance, and it gave me peace inside when not much else did—but nothing seemed to help for very long. Maybe I was just struggling to find my niche, or feeling the weight of falling short of my and other people's expectations, or just frustrated about a lot of things. But I started making different choices and hanging out with whoever accepted me.

As often happens, the people who accept you at that point in life are the kids who want to be different. I felt like I fit in with the people who made it a point not to fit in.

I started dating a guy during junior high, and it didn't matter to me that my parents didn't like him. "Kyle" was pretty rough around the edges—kind of your average skateboarder, dressed in jeans and a T-shirt with constantly messy hair—and his parents let him do whatever he wanted. He wasn't a good student, and my parents could tell that my attitude was changing the more I was around him. I was becoming more stubborn, rebellious, and rude. I did what I wanted to do whether my parents were okay with it or not. At one point, my parents told me I couldn't hang out with him anymore, so I said "okay" and then went over to his house anyway to hang out with him. It was clear that I was really started to change.

I had opportunities not to go down that path. One of my friends was a good influence. We did everything together for a while, and that could have turned me back in a better direction. But my other friends were still very much a part of my life—one of them, who I was very close to, got pregnant in eighth grade—and, of course, I was still dating the guy my parents didn't want me to date. Even though there were people who could have been a better influence on me, I spent most of my time with people who weren't.

I often had to hide the fact that I was going to see Kyle, but that didn't stop me from seeing him anyway. We liked each other throughout most of junior high. I knew he was probably going down the wrong path, but we had a ton of fun together, and there was never any fighting or yelling. We were in love as much as junior high students can be in love. I thought it was a great relationship.

I wasn't sure whether my parents had a good relationship at this time. When they got along, life at home was great. But they didn't always get along. For one thing, in addition to traveling with my little brother for hockey, my dad traveled a lot for work. After being a policeman for a while, he began working for the licensing and resource business Pops had founded and still ran, so Dad was on the road all the time for the company. He went back to being a police officer later, but during this time he just wasn't always around.

But I remember my parents fighting a lot when he was there, and that went back even to when I was little. I'm not sure what their arguments were about, but I can remember times when he was really mad. I was still pretty young when I asked my mother why she was married to him if it was so much trouble. I love my dad, of course—I always have—and he can be a very loving person. But we butted heads a lot during this time. And even though my mom and I usually got along pretty well, she and I were having our ups and downs too. I was really rude to her sometimes, and she let me know it. I got a lot of punishments that I know I deserved. A lot of these issues were typical family struggles, but they still felt unsettling.

Zeeland's two public high schools are very unusual. Zeeland East and Zeeland West are right next to each other and share some of the same facilities and classes. Students know each other and go to the same parties, but the two schools have different sports teams. They are both great schools that parents want their kids to go to.

I went to Zeeland East. So did some of the same friends I had in junior high. But something happened in high school, and those friends and I didn't get along like we used to. I remember having some arguments, though I'm not sure what they were about. Maybe a boy was involved, but I don't remember any details. I just know that some mean girls who used to like me didn't like me anymore, and mean girls can be relentless. I tried hard to make friends and to do well in school—I wanted high school to be different from the troubles I'd been having in junior high—but for whatever reason, these girls kept harassing me, and they wouldn't let up. We fought all the time.

About halfway through my freshman year, I went to a basketball game with a good friend who was a little older than me. As she and I were sitting there at the game, the girls I didn't get along with came over. They had pretzels and cheese, and some of them started to wipe the cheese all over me. We had never been violent toward each other at all, but I think they saw an opportunity to do something mean and took advantage of it. My friend and I decided it would be best if we left, so we got up and walked out. But they followed. When we got outside, they hit me—still with cheese in their hands—and punched me on my back. Our feud had turned into a full-scale physical assault.

I was crying and shaking, and I could tell I had bruises all over my body. Even in the moment, my self-hatred started speaking to me again. What had I done wrong? Why was I not enough for people? Why would people who used to be my friends hate me so much that they would attack me? I couldn't figure out why they were so hostile, but it definitely reinforced the self-image that had been forming in me.

My friend took me home, and I told my parents what happened. It was so bad that my dad took pictures of everything—all my lumps and bruises. We decided not to press charges, but it led to a conversation with the school. I wasn't involved in that; my parents talked to school administrators and handled everything at that level. But it became clear that I was not going to do well in that environment and that I should not continue going to Zeeland East. Within a couple of weeks, I was attending Holland Christian High School. I had only made it half a year at Zeeland.

I was really nervous about starting at a new school. I had no idea what it was going to be like and wondered if I'd have the same trouble with classes that I'd been having at public school. But it was amazing. I loved it. I met a great group of friends and was having a really good time. I generally had a ton of guy friends and not many girlfriends, but I got in with a group of girls who made me feel better about myself.

School still wasn't easy for me, and I was in special classes for my learning disabilities at this point, but I actually started doing well in them.

One teacher in particular became really involved in my life trying to help me get through everything I was dealing with. But my friends never mocked me or made me feel different because I wasn't in the same classes with them. They were my friends simply for who I was.

I had not felt welcomed with open arms in social groups like that before. As soon as I walked into the school, these girls made me feel at home. Just the fact that they were my friends made me feel better about myself, but a lot of what we did together built self-esteem too. We did makeovers together, they talked with me whenever I was down, and they would tell me encouraging things about myself. We'd go out after school, go to the beach, go to church . . . we did everything together. They were really good girls with their heads on straight, and I was having a ball. I thought life was starting to turn in a good direction for me.

At the same time, I was dating a guy from a different school—another boyfriend my parents didn't like for many of the same reasons they didn't like the first one from junior high—and I was enjoying life with him too. I thought he was a sweet guy. "Brandon" had long hair, was very tall and thin, and always wore jeans and a T-shirt, and he just didn't fit the image of the kind of guy they wanted me to be with. He also didn't think much of school and ditched classes often. My parents didn't want me following that same path and repeating a grade. They were hoping Holland Christian would be a completely fresh start for me. And they didn't think Brandon was very nice to me either. At one point when I got caught shoplifting a pregnancy test, they were adamant that I should end the relationship. But I convinced them that he was changing, that he wouldn't be a bad influence on me, and

that we were going to be fine. Like I always told them, "I've got this."
I had the confidence that I would continue to decide to thrive, but I
don't think I cared very much whether my parents liked him. I was a
teenager, and their opinion wasn't a big deal to me, though I wish it
had mattered to me more.

But my friends' opinions did matter to me, and they didn't think
Brandon was good for me either. Even though they and he never did
anything together—I kind of had a school life and a boyfriend life that
were separate from each other—they knew there were times when I'd
cry because he said something that made me feel worthless. I didn't
listen to them enough to break up with him—not yet anyway—but I
knew he probably wasn't best for me. But I thought I was very much in
love, and he said he felt the same way.

I was developing a pattern that would become common for
me—falling in love with how a guy made me feel, enjoying the thrill
of it, and then following blindly even after becoming disenchanted
with the relationship. Like so many people tend to do, I was always
trying to fill a void with my relationships, and the guys I dated always
made me feel like I was enough—at least for a while. Looking back, I
can see that I picked boyfriends who didn't really build me up at all.
One time I was riding around with a boyfriend and saw my dad, who
was policing that day, and for some reason I can't remember, we
ducked so he wouldn't see us and then tried to lose him. I knew I was
pushing the boundaries of what my parents and friends thought was
best. But the "bad boy" types in particular could talk like they were
so in love with me, and for someone who hated herself, it was what I
needed to feel.

As far as I knew then, things were going really well, and for the first time, I was doing well in school. But when I was 16, during my third year there, I found out I was pregnant. I was terrified.

I tried to tell my mom I was pregnant, but she wouldn't believe it.

"No you're not," she kept saying.

I told her I had already taken two tests at my friend's house, but she said I must not have been doing it right. So we went out and bought a pack of five pregnancy tests and brought them home. Same results. That still wasn't enough.

We went out a second time to get more, and she still could hardly believe it. First she was sad, then she was mad, and then she told me I would have to tell my father as soon as he got home from my brother's hockey game.

I was really scared about telling my dad. If Mom was taking this hard—and she was supposed to be the easier one to tell—I could hardly imagine how he would react. The night before, I had gotten a ticket for not stopping at a stop sign out in the country, and he had lost it. He talked to me like I was a criminal and told my mother I was never going to succeed if I kept acting like I had been. He was so mad. If he was acting like my whole life was going to go downhill over just one ticket, how would he react to this news? I was absolutely terrified to break the news to him.

Dad got home, and immediately Mom said, "Your daughter needs to talk to you. Go downstairs."

When he came into the room, I just sat there crying and shaking, so scared that it was hard to get the words out. But when I told him, he was eerily calm. It was something I had never experienced from him.

The first words out of his mouth were, "It's okay. We're going to make this work."

That was not at all what I expected to hear, and it made me feel understood. He and I had not gotten along very well recently, but his reassurance meant so much to me. He made me feel safe.

But there were more people to tell. The school had a rule for situations like this. You had to go before the board and apologize for your sin, knowing that it would result in being kicked out of the school. So I was really nervous about my next steps.

I told my gym teacher first, and he went and talked to the principal. The next day, it was over. I wouldn't have to go before the board after all. I wasn't sure what had happened or what kind of conversations they had, but they told me it was okay. They said they would support me and told me to let them know what I needed.

I was the first pregnant student at the school who was not made to apologize.

The idea of becoming a mother was scary. I had fears of going through it all by myself because I was worried I wouldn't be able to stay with Brandon. Things were changing between us, even before my pregnancy, and they continued to get worse. He had actually been excited when we first found out, but we were growing apart. And to be honest, something inside me wanted change. We fought all the time, and sometimes he verbally abused me. The fact that I had gotten pregnant added to his negative attitude toward me and that continued to feed my self-hatred.

It was definitely weird being pregnant in high school. People's responses, for the most part, were positive. Because Holland is such a religious community, I expected a different outcome, but people at school wrapped their arms around me and my situation. My friends and my teachers were all very supportive, which was so comforting and I appreciated so much.

That didn't take all the feelings of shame away; you can still feel like you've done something wrong even when people are supporting you, and I knew I had made a mistake. But my friends were excited about the baby and gave me a shower. They assured me they would be there for me throughout the whole process, and they were. I kept going to classes as usual, and my daughter wasn't born until near the end of the school year, so I didn't have to miss too much school. But I knew life would be different from then on.

Alison was jaundiced when she was born, so we had to leave her in the hospital overnight. That was really hard, and I started crying when it came time for us to go home. Brandon kept saying hurtful things to me, calling me a baby and telling me I shouldn't be acting that way. I was 17, a new mother leaving my child in the care of others, and he thought I was overreacting. It was too much for me to take, and I broke up with him on the spot. We had been very much in love with each other, had some really good times together, and had dreams of staying together and raising this child. But at this point, he was not very supportive at all, which was not a good sign for the years to come. It was really hard to do, but I ended our relationship before we even left the hospital.

I had the summer to recover before starting school again, and when the next school year started, it definitely wasn't easy trying to be a mother and a student at the same time. But people at the school did support me all the way through, just like they said. One time the daycare worker wasn't there when I tried to drop my daughter off in the morning, so the staff let me bring her to school, and they all took turns watching her while I went to class. They treated Alison like she was part of the school family.

There were some less supportive reactions too; one teacher kept telling me that what I had done was wrong in God's eyes and said I should have had an abortion. One of the assignments for her class was to take care of a fake baby for a week—it's supposed to help students know what the responsibilities of being a parent are like—and she gave me two choices: like the other students, I could take care of a fake baby (in addition to my own real baby), or I could write an essay on why I should not have had my child. I struggled with her condemnation a lot—and with the detentions she gave me. But she was the exception. Most people were very helpful and encouraging.

The love you have for a child is different from anything in the world. I absolutely loved my daughter. Being with Alison and taking care of her was extremely rewarding. And it seemed to turn some things around for me. Soon after I had her, I started dating a guy from school, and my parents loved him. "Jason" seemed to have every-thing figured out. He did well in school, he was planning to go to col-lege, and he treated me well. I had never had a relationship like this before. I had only dated the rough guys who were fun to be with but weren't very motivated at school and didn't have much direction. Jason was on the football team, had mapped out his future pretty clearly, and was very family-oriented. In fact, we did almost every-thing with his family. Both he and they were very accepting of me and my daughter. It was the first time I felt like I belonged and had something going for me. As far as I could tell, even in spite of having a baby at a time in life when most people are just enjoying being teenagers, life was still looking up.

Do You Need Immediate Help?

For Immediate help,
call the 988 Suicide and Crisis Lifeline,
available 24/7.
https://988lifeline.org/media-resources/
"If you or someone you know is experiencing a mental health or
substance use crisis, call or text 988"

chapter

3

Broken Relationships and Dreams

Jason and I dated throughout the next school year. He seemed to have everything figured out—he wanted to be a teacher and was planning to go Grand Valley State University when he finished high school. I was pretty surprised when he first asked me out. I wasn't exactly a typical student anymore. Why would a guy in high school want to take on the whole package—me and my baby—when he could have chosen a more typical life? Sometimes I asked him, "Are you sure you want to be doing this? It's a lot to go through."

But he always told me he loved me and had no fear over my situation. And he treated me very well, better than earlier boyfriends had treated me. As I mentioned, I was usually drawn to the bad boys who were on the verge of dropping out of school, and here was a guy who loved school and had a plan. And his parents were amazing too. They embraced me just as he did. Jason took me out on dates, helped with Alison, constantly told me I was enough for him, and encouraged me that I could do anything I wanted to do. For someone who felt like she never measured up, this was exactly what I needed to hear. He was constantly building me up.

So my senior year, in spite of being a little out of the ordinary, was a good experience. Jason, Alison, and I did everything together. I drank a little more that year and hung out with other kids who were doing that too, but not to a point that was unusual for high school seniors. We were just having a good time. My parents had the normal concerns that you would expect for that stage of my life, and of course having a baby made things a little more complicated for all of us. But they loved Jason and thought he was a wonderful boyfriend, and of course they loved Alison, and everything seemed to be heading in the right direction.

Jason graduated and went to college, and I would go see him on campus sometimes. I could get back and forth easily because Pops had bought me a nice, new car—a Jeep Grand Cherokee with nice leather seats—before I graduated from high school. He was always showing me how much he loved me, and I was really excited and very thankful.

For a while, things still seemed to be going well with Jason. But on one of my visits after he had been there a few months, we had a conversation that changed everything. Alison and I had just spent the night on campus, and the next morning he told me that he had come to the realization that we were headed in different directions. I'm not sure what changed, exactly, but he was no longer seeing us together for the long term. He wanted to break up.

I was stunned. I remember picking up Alison, getting my stuff together, and walking back across campus crying, wondering what had happened.

I felt like I'd lost everything. Again that thought resurfaced: *I'm not enough.* Even for someone who had told me again and again that I was enough, I wasn't.

I took our breakup extremely hard. It made me feel like I would never be enough—always unloved, unwanted, and worthless. I didn't have any motivation, I didn't know where I was headed in life, and I was feeling estranged from everyone.

Jason was right. I was definitely going down a different path from everyone else. It wasn't that long ago that I felt like everything in my life was going well. Now I felt like everything was starting to spiral downward.

I had felt like I was in love with my first two boyfriends, but looking back I know those weren't real love. But I thought my relationship with Jason was true love. I didn't think it was going to end, but it had. My whole life seemed to crumble before me. I was alone and didn't know what I was going to do.

My feelings of self-hatred grew stronger over the next few months, and I was very angry at life. I started to drink more, mainly as a way to cope. I had been accepted to a medical assistant program in Grand Rapids, and not long after I got there, I got in with the wrong crowd. At first, I was doing pretty well in classes, and I enjoyed being there. But I started to party a lot with my new friends—a totally different crowd from what I had known in high school. We would drink almost every night, and I spent much of school feeling hungover.

That made school harder and harder, for obvious reasons, but I was still feeling such a void in my life that I needed to fill it with something. Friends and parties seemed to do that for me.

At some point during this time, I got into a relationship that turned out not to be a good experience. We fought all the time, and it was just a horrible relationship from the start. One time, we decided to go to Maryland to see some of his friends, thinking we might move there with them, and we got in an argument. He left, and I didn't have a way home. He eventually came back and got me, but it's another example of not making the best decisions. I broke up with him as soon as we got back to Michigan. But I still looked for ways to fill the void with friends and good times.

Of course, I was in a different situation from most of my friends. I had a daughter at home. There were times when I called my parents to say I was going to stay out studying and would go out drinking instead. But I think they recognized what was going on pretty quickly. I quit giving that excuse and just called to tell them I wasn't going to come home. I could hear the disappointment in their voices, and I understood it. I was disappointed in myself. I didn't want to miss out on being with Alison. But I also had this sense of emptiness that needed to be filled and a lot of pain that needed to be soothed—my emotions kept going up and down—and I didn't have the tools to deal with any of that. So several nights a week, I would let my parents know I wasn't going to be there.

My parents were very concerned, although they had no idea of the direction I would go in the coming months and years. They knew I was strong-willed and always wanted to do my own thing, so they believed I eventually would make the right decisions—that I would stand up against bad influences. But they did tell me many times that I was going down the wrong path and wanted to know what they could do to help.

On nights when I was home—maybe a couple nights a week—we had this conversation often. They wanted to know what was going on, and they let me know they didn't like my friends or what they were doing to my life. In some ways, that just made me want to hang out with them even more. I'd get angry whenever we talked because I didn't want to be confronted with what I already knew was wrong. But the only way to avoid that confrontation was to stay away even more. Eventually that turned into not coming home at all.

To their credit, my parents never placed any conditions around taking care of Alison. They never used her as leverage against me. But they did make it clear that if I was going to continue to live that way, they were not going to try to protect her because they didn't want her experience of her mom to be off and on like that—seeing me one night, then not the next, here again and then gone again. I completely understood that. I wanted to protect Alison from that too. I had started dating a guy named "Shane" from my group of friends in Grand Rapids, and he and I got an apartment there together. I saw my daughter less and less often.

It didn't take long for me to find out that my friends were doing more than drinking—a variety of drugs, including cocaine and heroin, which I discovered by finding a needle in Shane's pocket. I didn't want to go to that extreme. I just went out and partied with them, getting drunk and not remembering much of anything the next day.

I eventually graduated from school with my degree, but barely. With all the partying, I had done just enough to pass the test.

I had been diagnosed with endometriosis before Alison was born, and it had continued to give me some problems since then. It hadn't always been constantly painful, but it had flared up enough for me to have surgery for it. But as I neared the end of school, it lasted longer when it came, and it got worse—to the point where I couldn't get out of bed sometimes. I felt pain in my lower abdomen, and it would shoot toward my back, which made me feel very tired. I'd feel like I had a fever with it sometimes too. Some days, I just wanted to load up on Tylenol, or something stronger if I had it, and keep a heating pad on. And even though that would help, doctors had not been able to prevent the episodes of pain.

That came to a crisis one night when a cyst burst, and I had to go to the hospital. It was incredibly painful, but they couldn't do much for me at the hospital. They gave me some pain meds, and after a while they sent me on my way. I didn't have any lasting solution for the pain I had been feeling—just a little relief that I knew would be temporary. I felt so down, so disappointed, and so hopeless. I thought I would always be dealing with this pain, and it scared me. I had gone to the hospital thinking I'd get help, and now I felt lost, like no one understood what I was going through and couldn't help even if they did.

That's when Shane decided to take matters into his own hands. He took me home from the hospital to our apartment in Grand Rapids, loaded up a syringe, and injected me with heroin. Within about twenty seconds, my whole body felt warm. I felt completely relaxed, and all my pain went away.

I hadn't felt that good in a long time—or ever, actually. I felt like I was in a place where low self-esteem, fear, and sadness did not exist and never would.

There were no responsibilities, no problems, no disapproval from anyone.

I didn't have any concerns about anything.

It was like heaven. I felt like a million dollars. And for the next couple of hours, I was at peace.

As soon as it wore off, everything came back—all the pain, fears, and disappointments. I felt all the weight of everything I had done and all the things that made me sad, just like before. But now I knew what it was like not to feel those things, and I wanted to get back to that peaceful place. I didn't know at the time that I'd never have that exact same feeling again—that the first use is unique. That's a big part of addiction—chasing that first time again and again. But right then, I just knew that I had gotten a brief taste of a heavenly, pain-free life, and I wanted more. I fell in love with it right away.

I was hooked.

For a brief time after I finished school, I worked as a home nurse. I was going back and forth from Grand Rapids to Holland to take care of a client, and one time Shane dropped me off at the job site in Holland, planning to come back and get me when my shift was over. But he got so high that he forgot me, and when I finished working, I didn't have a ride. I wasn't sure what to do, so I called Jason. He picked me up and took me back to where I was living in the drug house.

I was becoming very addicted during this time, and I had a hard time keeping a job. Even though I could never match that first high, heroin still felt great. It had taken less than a week to get hooked, and since everyone around me was doing it too, I had no reason not to keep on. I started doing it several times a day—Shane and I got up to around a gram and a half each day. Whenever I came back down, I'd go a couple of hours before the next hit, but I always felt like I was completely tied to it, like there was no way out. This was just how it was going to be, like I was carrying around a ball and chain that didn't feel heavy when I was high but always pulling me back when I wasn't.

And every time I did it, I knew I was further and further away from being able to be with my daughter. I felt dirty from what I was doing and guilty for letting my family down.

It led to a literally dirty life too—Shane and I couldn't keep up with rent and ended up living in a drug house with several other people. So we'd have random people sleeping there, and it was a very unclean and unsafe situation. I started to feel very isolated and alone, even though there were always people around, and I knew this was not a good life. But that just made me want to escape even more. And the only way I had to escape was to get high for a couple hours at a time.

We never had trouble getting our drugs. We had a dealer who was always loaded. We had trouble paying for them sometimes because using can be very expensive. We learned all kinds of ways to steal and sell things, cheat the system, and get by however we could. But heroin was never hard to find.

I felt like I was at a point of no return. I had started using because of my pain, but I think I would have gotten into it anyway, considering the people I was hanging out with. You can only be around a lifestyle for so long before it starts to become your lifestyle too. But I did have thoughts early on about trying to get out before I became any more addicted. I didn't want to miss seeing Alison or to disappoint my family.

One of the biggest warning signs that I was in too deep was my first overdose. I did some heroin and started to have an out-of-body experience, like I was floating. But suddenly my body started to shake, and I fell to the floor, completely blacked out. When I woke up, I was in a hospital—my friends had taken me there and left me at the door. I was told later that I had to be shocked back to life, but in that moment when I woke up, I was so mad that I wasn't high anymore that I ripped out my IV and walked right back to the house where we were staying, where everyone was using and acting like nothing had happened.

Almost dying should have been enough to turn me back. But even though I hadn't been in it very long, I didn't think I could get out of it. I also thought I was in love with Shane, and I didn't want to give him or my friends up. They were helping to fill a void, and I didn't want to leave the life I had with them.

But my parents kept trying to get me to come home. They told me they would help me however they could but that I needed to be with my daughter. They were disappointed in me, but they were also just very sad at what they were seeing. As a police officer, my dad saw this kind of thing every day. He knew what this lifestyle was like and what it led to. I know they were both in a lot of pain; I can't imagine what it's like to see your daughter going down the same destructive path you have to deal with on the job in law enforcement. And I think it scared them. My decisions were very hard on them.

Around this time, my Pops became ill with cancer and was no longer running his company. My parents left their jobs there. Mom wanted to teach again and began as a substitute teacher, and my dad was rehired at the police department where he had worked before. But often when my mom was called in to teach, she had to tell them no, either because I wasn't home or I wouldn't get up to take care of Alison. Eventually, she had to take her name off the substitute teaching list and focus more on caring for my daughter. My parents gradually took on more and more parenting responsibilities for her because I just wasn't around or in a condition to do it.

Mom and Dad had already sacrificed a lot. They spent a lot of time helping me study for tests to get me through the medical assistant program, and they had always been involved with taking care of Alison. They had watched me make questionable decisions, like selling the car Pops had given me for a smaller, cheaper car, then totaling that car in an accident and using the insurance money to buy something even cheaper and less reliable. For a while now, they had not known when or if I was going to come home at night. They kept waiting and hoping for a change, and they thought I might turn the corner once I graduated. But nothing changed when I finished school, and they decided to confront me.

They basically gave me an ultimatum. They told me that my lifestyle wasn't healthy for Alison, that I couldn't just keep coming and going as I pleased, and that if I was going to continue to stay with them sometimes, I would need to make some different decisions. They told me I needed to choose between being a parent and walking away. If I chose to stay, they said they would help me however they could. But they knew if I walked away, I might take Alison with me. They knew they were taking a big risk.

I don't think they expected me to walk out the door, but that's what I did. For me, life just seemed painful, and heroin gave me relief. I had gotten to a point of not caring about the direction I was headed.

But I cared enough about my daughter not to bring her into that lifestyle. I'd seen enough kids in the life I was going down, and I didn't want to put my daughter through that. So when my parents asked me to let Alison stay with them, I agreed. Their home was what she had always known, they had been with her for her whole life, and they wanted her to have some sense of normalcy. They were heartbroken over the choices I was making, and they wanted to protect Alison from them. If I wasn't going to be available for her, and since they had been taking care of her anyway, it made sense for me to give my parental rights to them. They and I both knew they were the best alternative for her.

I remember the night I gave mom the paperwork to sign. I know they were devastated that I was leaving but grateful I wasn't taking Alison with me. I knew it was important for Alison to be in a safe and stable home, and I knew I couldn't give her that. I had been very open about what I had been going through and how I didn't want it to affect Alison. They were more than happy to take her and keep her away from what I was going through.

Neither my parents nor I knew what the next couple of years were going to look like—how far things were going to go and how it would affect all of our lives. They would eventually seek out help to deal with it all. They wondered what they had done wrong and had to struggle with regrets about what they might have done differently. They reached out to an organization that helps families understand how addicts think. They had counselors come to their home to speak with them, my brother, and both sets of my grandparents, just so they could all be on the same page, and all were encouraged to respond to me in specific ways rather than just reacting to my decisions. They learned that for an addict, the drug is like their air—they fight for their next "breath" like it was a matter of survival, because emotionally it is. They learned how to empathize without enabling, to understand when their "help" wasn't helping at all. They had to learn how to say no.

That's one of the hardest things for families of addicts because saying no seems unloving. And to me, it was. I thought they were terrible for not helping me when I'd come to them for help, even though I had made the decision to walk away.

I'd get very creative in finding ways to manipulate and steal from them because when you're gasping for your next "breath," that's what you do. So my family learned how to empathize when I said I was eating out of a dumpster but not to help in ways that would feed my addiction. Sometimes my mom would call my doctors and tell them that if they prescribed certain medications, they were just helping my habit. Even though Mom and Dad were often in the dark about where I was and what I was doing, they tried to educate themselves however they could and respond to me in ways that would be most effective. They still got burned sometimes because I would still lie to them and they would believe me. Addicts learn to be very good actors. But my parents did their best.

But I didn't know any of this at the time. All of their learning about how manipulative drug addicts could be came well after I left home and gave over guardianship of Alison to them.

It was a terrible turn, but one I felt I had to make. Desperate people do desperate things, and I found myself in a lot of desperate situations over the next couple of years.

Leaving home was one of the worst decisions I ever made. But leaving Alison in my parents' care was one of the best.

Do You Need Immediate Help?

For Immediate help,
call the 988 Suicide and Crisis Lifeline,
available 24/7.
https://988lifeline.org/media-resources/
"If you or someone you know is experiencing a mental health or substance use crisis, call or text 988"

Life on the Streets

From a family's point of view, heroin addicts live in an underground, behind-the-scenes network of drug dealers and other users. It's like a subculture that users can step in and out of, and when they are in it, family members usually don't know where to find them or how to contact them. A user's personality changes over time, so my family didn't even know who I was becoming. But whenever I connected with them, they could tell I was no longer that confident, independent, feisty little girl they once knew. My attitude and my reasoning became unrecognizable to those who knew and loved me.

After I stopped going home and gave up rights to my daughter, I moved around a lot. I don't remember a lot of details about this period of my life because I was high so much of the time and either sleeping or just trying to survive the rest of the time. Usually a high would last for a couple of hours, and I tried to keep them going so there wasn't much time between them. I got up to a gram a day, sometimes a gram and a half, which is a lot of expense to keep up with. I was basically living from one high to the next however I could.

I lived in what we called a "drug house," where people like me stayed just to have a roof over our heads. It was an upstairs apartment with two bedrooms and six or seven of us there at a time, but visitors coming in and out too. It was a mess—junk all over the place, not much furniture, bad smells, hardly any food or anything to cover our basic needs. There was a point when we didn't even have toilet paper, so I had to use socks or shirts. If you opened the fridge, you might see a bottle of orange juice once in a while, but nothing else. It was just a place of survival. Homeless people would come stay with us all the time. We were focused only on getting our next fix.

One of the girls who lived there was named Cass. She was crazy. She threw herself down the stairs one time, mainly to get attention but probably also to get pain meds. Sometimes she would overdose just to get the attention she wanted. I guess she had a real need for it.

Her boyfriend was Chad. They both smoked crack, and he would get manic when he couldn't find his stash, tearing the house apart to find it, not realizing they'd probably just used it all. He was always going through garbage cans, flipping over the couch, looking in the dumpster, or wherever else he thought his stuff might be. I don't know how they came to live with us, but they ended up there for a while. Dealers came in all the time. It was a strange mix of people, and the place was nasty.

I don't know how we got by during that time. I think back to all the money we spent on drugs and how much I'd have today if we weren't using it all for that. However we did it, we managed a day at a time.

I couldn't hold a job because of the addiction. I couldn't work when I was high, for obvious reasons, and I couldn't work when I wasn't high because I would be dope sick—with withdrawal symptoms like body aches, nausea, hot and cold sweats, and all the emotional turmoil I was going through. I still don't know how we came up with all the money we needed to live and support our addictions.

For a while, I was able to get some money from a joint account my mother and I had together, but eventually the bank called her and told her what was going on—and that she could be liable for my bad checks—so she closed the account. Occasionally I'd go to my parents' house and get things that we could use or that I could sell, but going over there always opened up a conversation about trying to get help for me, which I didn't want to face. But I still did it sometimes when I thought I could get away with something we could turn around for drugs or profit.

Michigan has a low-income assistance program called "Bridge" that helps connect people with all kinds of local and state resources. Shane and a girl we were hanging out with each had one—all you had to do was go to the county office and prove that you had an income below the required level—so we would use those to buy food, sometimes for ourselves but also sometimes for our dealers. Sometimes I'd go to some fast-food place, pretend to be pregnant, and tell them they messed up my sandwich so they would give me a fresh one, and that's how we'd eat.

But we also stole a lot. We'd steal speakers, cameras, other electronics, whatever we could find. We got in a lot of trouble, but we found ways around it too. I never got caught; I just remember having a knot in my stomach all the time, knowing how wrong it was, but at the same time knowing I needed the drug. I was getting so sick that I felt like I had to do this. We'd steal from all kinds of stores, usually larger chain stores where it wasn't too hard to get out with a few hidden items. One time Shane found a bunch of copper with serial numbers on it—I think it was from a lot where a house was being built—and we spent all night burning it all down. Then we sold it to a recycling center in Grand Rapids. We would basically get what we could find and sell or trade it to get by from day to day.

I knew during this time that police were watching our house because one of my friends told me they were outside taking pictures one day. We had to be careful. It didn't really change what I was doing, but I did have to do it more cautiously. I didn't want to get caught. In fact, at that point I knew I wanted a better life and wanted to get out. But I also knew I couldn't. This was my lifestyle, and it wasn't getting any better.

Once when Shane and I needed more money for drugs, we took my car to a dealership to sell it. I had sold the beautiful Jeep Grand Cherokee Pops had gotten me several years earlier. I had it for a little while, but when I turned 18, I decided I wanted a smaller car. And since the title was in my name, I was legally an adult, and I could sell it if I wanted, I did. I went out and got something less expensive, much to my parents' and grandparents' disappointment. Then one night when I was in medical assistant school, I fell asleep at the wheel and totaled that car—my parents think I was under the influence, but I don't remember—and I used the insurance money to buy something similar. So I was two cars removed from the one Pops bought me. But the car I was driving was still made possible by that gift.

The owner of the dealership where Shane and I first tried to sell that car was Jeff Elhart, who lived in my grandparents' neighborhood and had helped Pops find the Jeep for me a few years earlier. I had not forgotten how generous Pops had been with that gift, and I knew he had given it to me because he loved me. I knew the car I was now driving was made possible because of the money I got from the Jeep. But in my addiction and desperate state of mind, that car became expendable. It just looked like a source of drug money.

When we tried to sell it at that dealership, the sales rep picked up on the fact something was wrong. As it turns out, he had once been an addict himself and could tell that we were high. He recognized the signs of addiction. He talked with Jeff, who tried to call my grandfather to let him know what was going on, and when they couldn't reach him, they ended up talking to my dad. They refused to buy the car from me.

Dad came down to the dealership. I think he saw this as an opportunity to bring me home, get me away from my boyfriend and that life, and get me some help, because I had actually been calling home during that period sometimes asking for help for various things. So he came not only to rescue the car but also to rescue me.

It was a bad scene. I was not looking for a rescue, and I called my dad some horrible names and told him I hated him and hated everyone and everything else too. He went home feeling broken and defeated, and he told Mom that they had lost me—that it seemed to be too late for me. It was one of the many low points for them during my time in a life of drugs.

My boyfriend and I drove off and found a dealership in Grand Rapids, about 40 minutes away, that would buy the car from us. We ended up selling it for way under its value—maybe for about $1,500, even though it was worth several times that amount. I no longer had a car, but I did have money for drugs and a vacation from our drug house and miserable lifestyle.

We stayed in a cheap hotel for three days and nights and bought a bunch of crack and heroin. We hardly left the room the whole time and just got high, drank, watched movies, invited some people over, and had a party. It wasn't even a nice room. The hotel was known for a lot of drug activity and prostitution, so it definitely wasn't a nice getaway kind of hotel. But it was still a huge step up from our place. For a few days, we had a decent bed, food, a bathroom, toilet paper, and everything else we wanted. It was a little break away from our hard life. We spent all we got on my car for less than a week of relief.

But it was over in a hurry. When we ran out of money, we had to go back to our house, and I felt horrible about it. We went back into the same situation as before—the drug house, fighting for drugs and having nothing, getting food however we could, just trying to get by. I wished we had spent the money on getting a new apartment or making a new start. The fact that Pops had given me the car that led to the one I sold, and that I practically gave it away for a few days of drugs, made me feel really guilty. But the need for drugs still outweighed the guilt—by far.

I did ask myself why I wasn't going home—why I couldn't just stop this crazy way of life and start a life for myself that would be better than what I was experiencing. I constantly missed home. I knew I had chosen drugs over my family, which even in my condition, I understood to be a bad trade.

I thought about how nice it was to be with family, play games, and have food and nice things to look forward to.

I thought about Mom and Dad and what they must be feeling. And I thought about Alison, of course. I missed her. I pictured what it would be like to kiss her again and hold her in my arms. Sometimes I talked to her on the phone, and I felt a constant battle going on inside me.

I just missed everything. I wanted to be so much more than where I was, but I didn't know the way out. I knew my parents were willing to show me a way out, but I didn't believe I could actually do it.

My grandparents called a few days later and told me how sad and disappointed they were about the car. Pops was always trying to protect me, and he kept asking what I needed. But I couldn't tell him, and there wasn't anything he could really do for me that would have helped anyway. GG, my grandmother from Chicago, called me often too, crying and asking me to come home, asking how I was doing and what I needed, always trying to help. I knew my family was heartbroken, and they were all very important to me.

I loved them very much. But I couldn't face up to my own pain and embarrassment or the pain I had caused them.

That was the biggest obstacle: the pain and embarrassment. I wanted out, and I thought about going back. I didn't know what that would look like or how I could do without heroin, and I didn't know how I could do without Shane either. I had become dependent on him. I couldn't imagine what his life would be like if I broke up with him.

Everywhere I looked, I felt guilt. There was no decision that would not also bring pain. I had already given up my daughter, and to go back to my family would have brought up all the embarrassment I felt and the embarrassment my family must have felt from what I had done. It seemed harder to go back than to stay away.

Later, my family made one last attempt to help me out with a vehicle when my parents bought me a moped for my birthday. They knew I need to get around town, and that's what they thought I would use it for. But I tried to ride it all the way to Ionia—about 60 miles away—to get drugs one time, and it broke down. After that, they told me they were done with helping me get around. I'd just have to take the bus from then on.

While we were living in the drug house, I found a baby kitten. I was absolutely in love with her because it was rare that I got to have something that was mine, and she was something I could care for and feel good about. So we went and got her some things to take care of her. But that night, she was cuddling with me and must have left to go into another room. Shane was having some kind of party with a bunch of people he didn't even know, so there were a lot of things going on and a lot of people moving around.

The next morning, neither of us could find the cat. I didn't know what had happened to her. But that afternoon, we found out when Shane went out to get us some heroin and found her behind the dumpster. My best guess is that somebody sat or stepped on her and decided to get rid of her. I was heartbroken. She had been a bright spot for me, but nothing good seemed to last for long in the life I was living.

My family made several attempts to get me back. My dad wanted to pick me up and take me to lunch one time, and I did want to have a decent meal, but at that point I didn't want him to see where I was staying, so I agreed to meet him at the restaurant. I knew he was hoping he could bring me home, but I kept telling him I was fine, that Shane and I were doing well. "I've got this," I told him. My parents came to hate hearing me say that because they generally knew it meant the opposite. Dad went home without me and with a heavy heart, but he and Mom knew I'd have to hit rock bottom before I'd even think about turning around. Little did I know that someday I would have to do more than decide to thrive—I would some day have to decide to survive.

They just didn't know how low rock bottom would be.

My grandparents from Chicago called one day and asked if they could come take me out to lunch too. I told them that would be fine. By then, they knew where I was staying and came and picked me up. We went out to a restaurant—a little old-fashioned style, nothing fancy, but with pretty good food. I was starving, so I ate whatever I could while I was there. We talked for a while, and then they started pleading with me to get out of my lifestyle. They promised to help me with whatever I needed, but the more they asked, the angrier I got. They actually wanted me to leave with them that day, but I just couldn't do it. So I got up and walked out.

They followed me down the road, begging me to get in the car. I had no shoes, but I just kept walking. I loved my grandparents—my GG meant the world to me—but I just couldn't get in the car and go with them. There were a lot of tears on both sides, but finally I just said no and left.

My grandparents went back to my parents' house, and everyone in the family was calling me and saying they would help me if I just came home. They pleaded as long and as hard as they could. But asking me again and again just made me madder. I don't know why—maybe because it was forcing me to face my guilt. I still wanted to go home, but I didn't feel like I could. I didn't want my daughter to see me that way. I would have had to be dope sick and deal with all those horrible withdrawal symptoms, and I didn't want to have to experience that. You feel like you're dying when you detox. But I also didn't want to face the embarrassment over everything I had done to my family.

Not long afterward, the police raided our drug house while Shane and I were out shopping. They arrested everyone inside for possession of all kinds of drugs—crack, heroin, cocaine. I think five people were there at the time and ended up being charged. When we came back, everyone was gone.

Shane and I weren't able to keep making our rent payments, so we were evicted. Just a few days before, I was walking home one night and found a man lying on the sidewalk. He was our neighbor who lived below us, and he was having some kind of seizure. I called 911, and that saved his life. He would have died if I hadn't seen him, so I'm glad we still lived there for that. But we couldn't stay there, so we went to live with Shane's mother for a while.

She could be very nice sometimes, but she had some mental health issues and could also be very hard to talk to, so you never knew what you were going to get from her. I loved her and wished I could help her, but sometimes that was hard to do. Sometimes she butted heads with him over his lifestyle—he was in and out of jail a lot, which she hated—but other times she didn't make an issue of it. We never could tell what state she was going to be in. She'd be fine one minute and screaming the next—very up and down as to whether she was sad or angry. So we only lived there for a little while, and even then we sometimes spent the night with his friends around town.

One night Shane ended up in jail for stealing something from a large store. He was wanted for almost the whole time we were together, so when he went to jail, we needed to get him out as quickly as possible, before the authorities realized there was a warrant out for his arrest. I went to our dealer and told him what was happening and asked for help. He said I would owe him—I'd have to run deliveries for him or give him rides wherever he needed to go with whatever car I could arrange to use—but he gave me the money for bail. I'm not sure how no one noticed the warrant, but Shane's mom and I got him out before they did.

Right away, we went and used. We jumped around from house to house, including living with his mom for a while or staying with friends sometimes. We didn't have a home; we just bounced around. It was the most unstable kind of life, and I never knew what to expect from one day to the next. I didn't know if I was going to live or die, and I really wanted to see my daughter, but I felt like such a messed-up mom that it didn't seem possible. Even though I wasn't far away from her, I felt like we were worlds apart.

Even though a new life that involved being off drugs and back with my family seemed out of reach, a new start within the life I was living didn't. Something had to change. I wanted Shane to get out from under the charges that he had been wanted for so they wouldn't be hanging over his head anymore. I thought that if we could get that off his plate, maybe we could move forward and have something of a more normal life—maybe find a place to live, have some stability, and get back on our feet. So we talked about him turning himself in. I hoped he would serve a couple months, get back out, and then we could have a fresh start.

I was kind of surprised when Shane agreed, but he did. He turned himself in and ended up serving time in prison. But it didn't go like I expected. He didn't serve for just a couple of months. He was convicted on charges that sent him away for about a year and a half. Shane was the love of my life then, and it was so hard to let him go.

Again, I was alone, and I didn't know what to do. I felt like I was out on the street to fight for myself. That idea of a semi-normal life seemed even further away. I went to stay with some friends, and we partied every night. I don't remember much of what happened during this period of my life because I was high all the time. I remember going to see Shane as often as I could and taking his mom to visit him once a week. And I remember being sick a lot. I got hepatitis C.

Hepatitis C is common among drug users because it spreads through infected blood, usually with shared needles. Its common symptoms can include joint pain, fatigue, loss of appetite, fever, nausea, and several other things. Some of these symptoms overlapped with drug use. My body was already tired and feeling a lot of pain—that's why living from high to high was so appealing in the first place—so I don't know if I was having symptoms of the virus or not. But I did know I usually felt sick if I wasn't high.

At that time, the treatments for hep C were injections that caused a lot more side effects than the pills used now. I felt terrible much of the time—the side effects, like nausea, hair loss, muscle and joint pain, fatigue, weren't much different from having the virus itself. I had to give myself injections at certain times of the day, and doing that while also trying to get high was really hard.

I felt like I was drowning. I was in so deep that I couldn't see the light.

I didn't feel like I was good enough to stop—like getting out of that life would have been too good for me, even if I knew where to start.

Do You Need Immediate Help?

For Immediate help,

call the 988 Suicide and Crisis Lifeline,

available 24/7.

https://988lifeline.org/media-resources/

"If you or someone you know is experiencing a mental health or substance use crisis, call or text 988"

Gasping for My Air

After Shane went to prison, I started hanging out with a friend named "Amanda." We had known each other for a while. She was a dealer's girlfriend, and even though her boyfriend was in prison like mine was, his brother still looked after her and took care of her rent. It was a good situation, and she and I started living together.

Amanda was full of life—very fun to be with, and a caring and loving person. I had spent so much time in relationships with guys that it felt nice to have a girlfriend to hang out with again. We had so much fun together, and life seemed almost normal again when I was with her. We'd go out to bars and let other people buy us drinks. We still needed money for drugs, but since her boyfriend had been a dealer, it wasn't too hard to get them. But mainly we'd just hang out, grab something to eat, and find fun things to do. At home, we loved watching movies, and sometimes we played board games. She had a son, so sometimes we would go to see him, and she came with me a couple of times to see Alison. It was awesome for me to see that side of her and for her to see that side of me.

In many ways, apart from the circumstances that brought us together and the fact that heroin was running our lives, it was a normal girl relationship.

We talked about going to get our nails done or how we wanted our hair done.

We talked about guys and what we wanted life to look like for us in the future—about getting out of the life we were in and what that would look like for each of us.

We wanted to get decent jobs and maybe have our own apartment together.

We dreamed about having a somewhat normal life. Just having good jobs and good guys with us seemed like a fairy tale. But it was something we both longed for.

One day, Amanda and I were both really dope sick. We went out to try to start the car to go to our dealer's cousin's house, but the car wouldn't start. We decided to walk to the store and get some gummy worms—you crave things like that sometimes—and on the way back, I saw a car shop and stopped to ask if I could borrow their jump box. They said that would be okay, so I grabbed it and carried it for about a mile and a half. It was so heavy, and I was so dope sick, but we got it home, and our car started right up.

Amanda had clients she slept with for money sometimes, and there was a time I started doing that too.

I felt awful about it. The first time, I had an internal argument about whether I should or shouldn't, but when you need money for drugs, the drive for that next high outweighs the internal battle. I had already let that drive separate me from my daughter and the rest of my family, and this seemed like just one more step further.

But I had immediate regrets. I constantly felt dirty about it, so I had to get high before doing it and then again afterward. I remember feeling such a letdown and so guilty.

One time when I wasn't with Amanda, there was a guy who took me to another guy's house to sleep with him, and there were three more there who wanted it too. I was supposed to be with one but ended up having to do it with all of them. It was a horrible way to get drug money, but we did this kind of thing a lot for a little while. But it didn't last long—I think we only did it for about a month and a half before several things happened that made it unnecessary—and I hoped I never had to do it again.

Pops and Gerks didn't know all the ways we were supporting ourselves, but they knew they weren't all good, and they wanted to help us out. Sometimes they would have Amanda and me over to spend the night. We'd help around the house with things like yard work, and Pops would pay us for it. I don't know if he thought giving us some work would help us get out of our lifestyle or if he and Gerks just wanted to stay in touch for whenever we were ready to get out, but it was something they could do for us. They and Mom would sometimes disagree about how much of their help was empathy and how much was enabling, but they were just trying to help us as much as they could.

I stopped going to see Shane in prison after a few months. It got to be too hard to see him and to go get his mom to take her back and forth, and he was going to be there a while. I also started going home sometimes, but I never stayed long. My parents were glad for me to come see Alison, and they still wanted me to come home for good. I wasn't willing to do that, but I did want to stay connected. I had mixed feelings; I wanted to see my daughter, of course, but I also didn't want her to see what I had become. Sometimes I'd come for a short time, and sometimes I would spend the night with them. It was very much an in-and-out relationship.

But I still always had dope on me. I was high almost all the time and hated everything about my life, but I was in so deep I couldn't get out. I was trying to have a foot in both worlds.

There were times during these years I could feel addicted to guys kind of like I was addicted to drugs. Heroin gave me a good feeling but was really bad for me, and some of the guys I dated had the same effect. The attention they gave me at first filled a void, but then I'd put up with mental and physical abuse hoping that void would remain filled. I might not have liked being with a guy, but I felt like I needed to be with somebody. Just being with someone, even if the other people in my life didn't approve of him, was a really strong pull.

But sometimes those two addictions came into conflict with each other. Amanda and I went to a bar one night and got pretty drunk, and I went home with a guy I met there. When we woke up in the morning, I told him I was a heroin addict. For a couple of days, he tried to get me out of it. He kept me from going out by myself, took me out to keep my mind off getting my next fix, made me soup when I started to feel sick, put me in a hot shower to help me feel better, and that sort of thing. It lasted for a few days, and he did his best.

He was a really decent guy—tall, strong, a Navy Seal, and a personality that just wanted to help. He had a good head on his shoulders. I could tell he felt so bad for me, even though we had just met. He saw potential in me. In a lot of ways, that made me feel really good. I felt safe and supported. He made me feel like maybe I could live a normal life—that maybe there was a chance for me to get out.

But now I had two forces pulling against each other—my need for my "air" and my need for a guy to fill the void in my life. I really liked this guy, but I also needed my drugs.

I also really wanted to go back to Amanda. She was my girl, my best friend, and I couldn't leave her.

Even with all the help this guy was giving me, I was still using. I wanted what he was offering, but I couldn't just quit. He thought he would be able to help me through withdrawal, but I didn't think I had the strength to go through that. When he found out I was still using, that was the end of that. He wasn't going to invest any more time in someone who wasn't going to make the effort. I lost a really good guy.

Amanda and I went to a party one night and were told later that we got in a fight with each other. Neither of us remembered anything about that night, but we ended up in our car together in the drive-way. Her boyfriend's brother came out of the house and found us and wasn't very happy about it. But we weren't upset with each other. We had no idea what we might have been fighting about. We still got along well.

Eventually Amanda's mom came and got her and took her to rehab. That didn't go over well with Amanda at first—it was a little bit of a scene—but she knew she didn't have much of an option. Her parents told her that if she wanted to see her son, she needed to get cleaned up. She had tried before. For many addicts, it takes several times of going through rehab before it finally clicks with them, if it is ever going to, and this would have been Amanda's fourth or fifth time. But she was going to have to try again.

And once again, I was left all alone.

I had nowhere to go and again felt very isolated. As hard as it was, I went back to live with my parents for a while. I had to work up the nerve to go back there. I knew they would welcome me home, but I also knew they would see it as an opportunity for me to make major changes and get out of my lifestyle, and I didn't have much hope that could happen. I expected that there would be a lot of conversations about getting me to stop using drugs. And there were. They kept asking how they could help me, they'd suggest certain rehab places that they could get me into, asking what I thought about this option or that option. I didn't think any of them would help.

My parents never did what Amanda's parents had done, telling me I couldn't see my child if I wasn't going to get clean, although there were times they told me I couldn't keep staying with them if I didn't stop using. But I knew they wouldn't kick me out. I had drugs with me when I was there, and I kept using, and even though I wasn't living up to what they expected, they let me stay. But I couldn't keep having those conversations. I was constantly in and out, never fully there. I'd go back and forth from there to wherever else I could find. I'd stay with my parents most nights but felt a lot of guilt for getting high in their home with my daughter right there. And the guilt just made me want to go deeper into using.

I had become close with my dealer—he and I were like brother and sister and got along really well, and I didn't have to sleep with him for my drugs, which made other girls hate me—and I'd stay with him sometimes and help him deliver for the day. But I had constant worries of getting caught. Making deliveries meant I had a lot of drugs on me at times, and I knew it was a risky situation. I didn't want to go to jail. I also worried about clients I was meeting with—strangers who might be dope sick or who wanted to take advantage of the situation and rob me.

One time I met up with some meth-heads at a store. They have a reputation for being really nuts and even in the drug world are considered pretty low on the food chain. I know they were like me in some ways, in their reasons for being addicted and in their need for help, so I felt for them. But it was always risky being around them. Usually when I met clients at a store, we'd go down an aisle and I'd be able to just hand them the drugs and get the money. It was supposed to be that simple because none of us wanted to get caught. But these meth-heads were acting crazy, like a lot of meth addicts do—nervous, moody, suddenly loud or violent. I was trying to give them the drugs, and they kept trying to talk to me and were even shouting things out. I don't know why they were calling attention to us, but it scared me. I ended up leaving without making the transaction because I just didn't want to deal with them anymore. Most of the time I was able just to go to a meeting spot, switch drugs for money, and call it done, but the possibility of incidents like this always made me nervous about getting caught.

By this time, I was in so deep and in such bad shape that even my dealer wanted me to stop. I was shooting up all the time, and my arms were looking terrible. I had huge, red bumps with pus coming out of them. They hurt and felt hot, and I knew they were making me sick. My arms were in so much pain, and I could hardly move them because of all the abscesses on them. They had gotten huge, and I was getting sick with fevers because of them.

One day when the dealer and I were out making a delivery, I pulled up my sleeves. He saw the abscesses and lost it. He told me this had gotten ridiculous and that I was going to die if I didn't get help. He said he was taking me home and would pay for rehab, and he refused to give me any more heroin until I saw a doctor.

That night, I went home to my grandparents' house—I had been staying with them for a little while during this time when I was bouncing around from place to place—and my uncle, my mom's brother, was living there too. He and I are very close. I always felt that I could tell him things I couldn't say to others because he had struggled with addiction himself. He had been an alcoholic, so he understood a little of what I was going through.

He would have the same conversations with me that other people would, asking how he could help, inviting me to meetings, just wanting to be available however I needed him. And I actually did go to a couple of meetings with him. But he was always understanding and never judgmental throughout all I had been through. I felt like I could trust him with all my secrets. I could literally tell him anything, and it would stay between us. I felt like we could figure out anything together. So after we had watched a movie, I told him I didn't feel very well.

"I don't know what to do," I said as I pulled up my sleeves to show him my arms.

My uncle ran upstairs, told my grandparents we were going out to a bar, and took me straight to the hospital.

I couldn't believe how fast they admitted me. I had a life-threatening infection. At first, they thought they might have to amputate my arms, but they decided instead to cut them open and see if that helped. The infection had reached my heart and kidneys too, so I had to be hooked up to antibiotics and pain medications. Of course, with all this going on, my uncle had to call my family and tell them what was happening.

My whole family came to see me. As I lay there, I had no choice but to hear everything they wanted to tell me.

My brother and his girlfriend were crying. "I need you to stop," he told me. "I don't want to lose my sister. I *can't* lose my sister. Please let us help you."

My parents told me how scary it was to almost lose their child—not just now, but the entire time I was doing drugs and out on the streets, wondering if they would see me again, hoping they didn't get a call about me dying or being arrested.

It was absolutely heart-wrenching to hear and see what I had done to my family, and to know how close to death I had been. I was high from the pain meds, but it was a clear-headed high, not like a heroin high, and I took in everything they said. I could see how much they still cared and how much they wanted to help. And if I was honest with myself, I knew I was worn out from living the way I had been living. Even in the moment, it seemed like a turning point.

And I thought, maybe for the first time ever, *I think I can do this. Maybe it's my turn to give it a try.*

Do You Need Immediate Help?

For Immediate help,
call the 988 Suicide and Crisis Lifeline,
available 24/7.
https://988lifeline.org/media-resources/
"If you or someone you know is experiencing a mental health or
substance use crisis, call or text 988"

High Hopes and Tragic Depths

As far as my parents were concerned, I was their captive for a brief moment in time in that hospital. They were paying my medical bills, they talked with the doctors every day, and so they saw this as their chance to get some help for me. I could tell how much they and the rest of my family still cared about me. And to be honest, I was glad to be in a place where I could rest for a while.

That doesn't mean I was always cooperative while I was there. I was given minimal doses of drugs, for obvious reasons, and I was very frustrated and angry that doctors and nurses weren't treating my pain like I wanted them to. My mom says I was extremely rude to the nurses, even though they were doing a good job taking care of me.

The hospital probably could have released me sooner than it did, but my parents kept negotiating with the doctor about my time there, asking him not to discharge me until they found a place for me in rehab. They knew if there was much of a gap between the hospital and rehab, I could have easily changed my mind and gotten out of it. So while I was still in a hospital bed, they kept working to get me into rehab and work out the financial side of things, which wasn't easy to do.

Once rehab was lined up, the hospital discharged me. But first I spent one night at home. I would be headed off to an addiction recovery treatment center about two hours away from my family in Brighton, near Detroit, the next day.

"I can't believe I'm cutting your hair in case you get in a fight in rehab," my father told me. I had extensions in my hair, and he was the only one home that evening, so he was cutting them out for me. That was his big thing—worrying that I might get in a fight. He had become very supportive recently, and our relationship was growing closer. He wanted to make sure I was safe.

I was really nervous the next morning. I didn't want to go. I wanted to be able to stay home and try to recover on my own. It was that independent streak I always had in me, plus a fear of going through a program I had no control over. But I did go, and I began the initial treatment process. It was a typical approach to rehab. They substitute a drug for a drug, so they put me on Suboxone, a medicine that treats narcotic addiction, as well as some other medicines for sleep and other issues. We had to attend classes three times a day and had different devotion groups we could participate in. They also had games we could play outside.

There were no individual sessions, but the group sessions were somewhat helpful. But I really didn't like being there. I didn't like having to say, "Hi, my name is Brittany, and I'm an addict." I felt like that kept reinforcing the mindset that I was an addict, and it puts people in a position of hearing everyone's sad stories over and over again. You're already feeling dope sick and don't want to be around people, but you still have to go to all the classes. And this was a very rough crowd.

My stay in rehab was typical in that insurance covers only 10 to 15 days and then cuts off. Of course, two weeks is not long enough for someone who has been addicted to heroin for a long time to establish new ways of thinking and behaving. I was off of drugs for a moment, but not to the point that anyone would consider me better or ready to be on my own.

My parents worked at getting me into outpatient treatment, the center's halfway house. They went to meetings beforehand to know how to work with me, learn how the brain works, and understand the medical and behavior aspects of recovery. They also had to figure out how to fund it, which meant pulling from pensions and other savings that made it a real stretch for them. Somehow, they made it work.

So after inpatient treatment, I was able to stay in one of the residences on campus as an outpatient. It still involved a lot of classes, as well as therapy sessions, arts and crafts, games, and other activities that helped keep us busy and develop different interests. We had to clean our room and keep up with basic responsibilities like that. I didn't get along with the other girls there, and I didn't like having to go to classes all the time. I found the rules to be very hard. I think the twelve-step approach can be helpful for a lot of people, but looking back, I don't think it addressed the root issues behind why I went down the road I did. I was making some progress, but I couldn't tell how much good it was doing, even though I convinced myself I was better now.

I met "Brian" there—he was staying in the men's residence—and we had a ton of fun together. We got to know each other really well. He had gone to rehab for Xanax and marijuana, and some drinking. He had never gotten in as deep as I was, but it was still an addiction he needed help for. But he and I both thought we were doing well in recovery, and after a couple of weeks, we decided we wanted to leave because we believed we would be okay on our own. I thought I was far enough away from my former life at this point that getting back into it wouldn't affect me. I was still on five different medications, and in reality, I knew I wasn't totally better. But I felt bored and wanted to get out of there, and this was my opportunity to leave.

My parents were totally against this, of course. When I called to tell them about my exciting new relationship and how great Brian and I were together, they were very clear that rehab was not a good time to fall in love with anyone. They kept telling me that I could still be with Brian after rehab if I wanted to, but that getting better was the most important thing for me right then, and the road to recovery was going to be a long and difficult one.

But I thought being with Brian was part of my journey of getting better—that we could make it with each other's help—and we got plenty of support from his mother. She thought we were doing great and told my parents that it would all work out okay. So when we decided to leave, Brian's mom came to pick us up to move in with her.

Brian was full of life and energy. He was constantly on the go. I remember having trouble keeping up with him because he was just so energetic. He loved life and was happy all the time. He was very loving and supportive, and he made me feel like I meant the world to him. We lived in his mom's basement and went out every day to do something. We stayed very busy. Sometimes we would go to NA (Narcotics Anonymous) meetings. Brian was a very good golfer—he could have had a future in the sport—so we went to the golf course often. I had never played golf before, so I drove the cart, and we'd stay and have lunch there. Sometimes we'd go drive around at a go-cart track, and since Brian loved baseball, we played and watched a lot of baseball. We'd watch movies at night, and I remember lying there being so in love with this special man. He was very different from the people I had spent the last few years with. It was a nice change.

I felt extremely happy and at peace—and loved. That's what I really wanted. I had gone years without feeling loved, and I often felt like whatever love I did experience was fake. This felt real. I had found my true love.

After a while, Brian and I decided to get married, and again my parents protested. I asked them to come to my wedding, and they said "absolutely not." They thought it was a horrible mistake, the unhealthiest thing two people in recovery could be doing, and pleaded with me to come home. Brian's mom kept calling my mom and telling her how terrible they were for not showing support for us. And I was angry with them too, not only because they didn't approve of our marriage, but also because they basically cut me off financially. They had just invested thousands of dollars in my rehab and were afraid it was all going to be undone. They had very little left to give and didn't want to keep pouring money into what they felt were bad decisions. I understand that now, but at the time, I was furious and stopped communicating with them very much at all.

Like the independent, self-sufficient little girl I once was, I was determined to do this on my own.

So Brian and I got married, and after a few months, his mom bought us a house so we could have our own place. We would still do things with his family, and I really felt at home with them. But living on our own, without the accountability of the recovery center and our families, we both started using again very quickly.

It started with drinking for Brian, but my dealer had also reached out to see if I could help get some stuff from his cousin in Detroit and deliver it to him. I didn't start using heroin again right away, but after a couple of weeks of delivering, it was a small step back into that old habit.

We were in a good place, and there really wasn't a reason for falling back into drug use. It wasn't a rational decision. It was just something to do. I just decided that this was my life, part of who I was, and the pull to get high was stronger than the resistance I had developed. I didn't have a rhyme or reason for why I did it. I just knew Brian had started drinking, smoking marijuana, and doing Xanax again, and those things were all around, so why not?

I knew at the time that I was giving up all my progress. I think Brian knew he was doing that too, even though I never asked why he was getting back into it. It was just something to do. It was what we knew. So he went back to Xanax, marijuana, and alcohol, and I went back to heroin—our same old habits. We were in Detroit now, so I didn't have the same supplier, but because my dealer's cousin lived there—in an even rougher neighborhood than the ones I'd lived in—and because I had already been delivering for him, I continued working with him.

I continued going on some supply runs between Detroit and Grand Rapids for my dealer and his cousin. I'd go on one- or two-day trips, sometimes bringing things to other people, but mainly driving back and forth to pick up and deliver between them. I'd get all my drugs for free for making the runs. They made us feel like a tight-knit little family. We'd go to parties with them, and they'd come over to our house, and it seemed like we had a good thing. But it was still right back into a rough kind of life.

The danger of that life was made real to me on several occasions. One time I went to meet a girl in Detroit because she was lost and didn't know where my dealer's house was. We met at a gas station on Eight Mile Road that happened to be on another dealer's turf, and he thought I was making a move on his territory. As soon as I saw his guys, I yelled to this girl to get out of there.

The next thing I knew, the guys were grabbing me and beating me.

I remember seeing only blood and feeling like I was going to die.

I could feel them rape me, and I was barely conscious when they left me for dead behind the gas station.

Living in the world of drugs isn't easy for anyone, but it especially isn't easy for women. We're vulnerable to all kinds of risks. I went through beatings on several occasions and had to endure rapes like the one behind that gas station, and as I mentioned earlier, there were times when I had to have sex with a dealer or allow him to pimp me out. It was brutal. But when you're gasping for your "air," you put a lot on the line just to get that next breath.

One night about six months after Brian and I had gotten married, and not long after we had moved into our house, we were home watching TV together. We loved shows on Animal Planet, and he was being his usual self—happy and full of life. Everything was a joke for him, and we were just having fun together. My dealer stayed with us sometimes, and he was there that night too—like I said, one happy family. Before we went to bed, I decided to take a bunch of heroin and of course passed out after that. I was completely out of it until morning.

When I woke up in the morning, I felt like I needed another hit, so I did a quick shot. Then I looked around and saw Brian lying on the floor. What a night. He had passed out too. So I called to him to get him to wake up, but he didn't answer. I thought he must still be really out of it. I kept calling and trying to wake him up, but he still didn't respond.

Finally, I went over to where Brian was and saw that he was cold and blue. I knew immediately that he was dead.

I started screaming and crying and didn't know what to do. I felt so lost and hurt.

I wished it was me.

My dealer was still there with us, and I think he was in shock too. Then a detective came. And then I had to tell Brian's mom what had happened.

She was heartbroken, of course. And furious. Right away, she started spewing a lot of hate and anger. She had no idea Brian had gone back to using again. She had been assuming he was still clean, so this was a huge shock to her.

"You killed him," she kept saying. In her shock and anger, she told me that it was all my fault, and that I shouldn't be there. I shouldn't even be alive.

And obviously I had a ton of hate toward myself, as I always had. I felt like this was my fault, and she made it clear she thought it was, even though I didn't have any idea what had happened.

I didn't know what to tell her.

Had Brian used my stuff? He never used heroin, so I didn't think it could be that. And I don't know why he would try it without me being there and awake to help him.

But that's what it was. Heroin had killed him. The detective questioned me, and I thought I might get charged with possession of heroin, morphine, and marijuana, even though the marijuana wasn't mine. I could have ended up with all the possession charges for everything. They took me to holding, and I talked to my dad on the phone. Being a cop, he gave me advice on what to say and what not to say, and I didn't feel like talking much anyway. And there really wasn't much I knew how to explain.

Over the next few days, the detective called our house several times and asked to talk. Dad kept telling me that legally I didn't need to talk to him and recommended that I didn't. He talked with the detective several times, told him to stop calling me on the phone, and asked all the right questions. Did the detective want me to come in? Did he have a warrant? What was the plan? We wanted to go by the book, but there was no warrant and they didn't call me in, so there was nothing to say at that point.

Meanwhile, my parents were dealing with Pops, who was very ill by that time. It was clear that he was not going to last much longer. They also had two foster kids at their home. Taking care of Alison had made them aware of how many other children out there are in similar situations but don't have grandparents or other family members nearby to take on the responsibility of parenting them, so they decided this was one way they could help others. So they had a lot going on—talking with hospice nurses about how to care for Pops in his final days, juggling that with a home life that now included three children, and now their daughter in crisis, clearly using drugs again and finding her husband dead from an overdose.

Because my parents had foster children and had to follow certain guidelines and regulations, they could not have a drug-using daughter coming to stay in their home. So they asked my grandparents from Chicago if I could stay with them for a while, again checking to make sure there were no warrants out for me before letting me go out of state.

Grandpa and GG came to pick me up as soon as they could. Brian and I had gotten a black lab together, and I remember holding that dog all the way back to Chicago. It felt like the last thing I had that I could hold onto. I felt so sick. I couldn't see anything but Brian's face. The guilt, the pain, the fear, the loneliness—it was all so much. I was also feeling physically sick—the endometriosis flared up again, and I actually had surgery for it again the week I stayed with them in Chicago.

I felt horrible. My world was shattered.

During that week in Chicago, I found out how sick Pops actually was. His battle with cancer had been going on for a while, and it looked like things were getting close, so my Chicago grandparents brought me back to my Zeeland grandparents' house. When I got there, my grandfather wasted no time in telling me what he wanted.

"Do not go into the streets anymore," he said. "Use my pain medicine."

He was on morphine, and he knew that would be safer for me than getting drugs from the streets, so he wanted me to use his stuff. It wasn't just about my next fix, though. He didn't want me doing what I had been doing anymore.

It was really hard to see my grandfather so sick. We had always been very close. I wanted to do what he said, so I did use some of his medicines, but I would also go and get drugs from my old dealer as well.

What I didn't know was that my parents had been talking to a friend from high school and his family about a treatment center in Argentina. My friend had struggled with addiction too. He had become a supplier, and he sold some drugs to another student who died, so he was charged with possession and cause of death. I can't remember how much time he served, but when he got out, he went to this place in Argentina, and it changed him.

My parents had been having meetings with people who were all associated in one way or another with this treatment center. They knew it was very different from the rehab center I had already been through— that they did not use any drugs to help with detox and withdrawal, that they did not see addiction as a disease but as a result of self-image and perceptions about life, and that they had a really high success rate, more than 99 percent for people who go through the whole treatment plan.

But they also knew it was very expensive. They would need to get outside help in addition to pulling from more of their own resources. But they were desperately hoping something would work and were thinking this might be the last shot I had at breaking the addiction, or even remaining alive for much longer. They wanted to do whatever it took to make it happen. They also started trying to figure out how to get me to want to go.

When my parents mentioned this treatment center to me as a possibility, I said no. Didn't even think about it. No way I was going to Argentina. They told me it was different from anything else, and my friend was a great example of how it could help, but I wasn't having that.

I don't recall exactly what I was thinking at this point—things had been so traumatic, and the drugs weren't helping my memory either. So I either can't remember all that happened during this time or I chose somewhere along the way to block it out. But I think I assumed I wasn't worth the help.

Deep down, I thought I was too far gone, although they remember me trying to convince them that I was going to get better on my own. "I've got this," I said to them once again. In reality, I might have been open to it if I thought it had a chance of working, but I don't think I even considered that a possibility. Plus, Argentina is a long way away. I had no idea where it was, but I knew it was far from home. It just seemed out of the question.

Pops started to deteriorate very quickly. My family and I were at his and Gerks' house for dinner one night, and I just had this feeling he wasn't going to make it much longer, so I said so.

"He's going to die tonight," I told them.

They thought I was high, and actually I was, but that wasn't what was making me think what I was thinking. I told them he was going to die that night, and the next morning, he did.

I talked to my grandfather right before he died, and with his last breath, he asked me to go to Argentina. I couldn't tell him no, so I said I would at least give it a try. I didn't want to do it, but this was my grandfather's last wish. I promised I would try.

I was so angry with myself. This was not what I wanted, but I couldn't tell Pops no. I had made a promise, and either I was going to have to go or find a way out. And the only way out seemed to be death.

After somebody dies, hospice comes in and takes all the morphine and other drugs that a patient was on, but I had taken most of it before they got there and put it away. So I loaded up two syringes of heroin and two of morphine and put them in my veins. I had actually tried to overdose on heroin a few days before, but this time I was going to make sure I took enough to end my life. I felt like God had taken everything from me—Brian and my Pops, two of the most important people in my life, gone within a couple of weeks—and I didn't see any way up from there. I was too far gone in addiction, I didn't want to go to rehab and didn't think it would help, and I didn't have any more hope of a normal life or anything good happening.

Like Brian's mother said, I shouldn't be here. And if I was responsible for Brian's death, it was only fair to take my life too. So I made sure to shoot myself up with enough to end it all.

I have no idea why it didn't work. The amounts I took should have killed me, but they didn't. I still don't understand why. I blacked out a little bit, but I was fine, and I was able to go upstairs and talk to my grandma. I have no explanation for how that happened.

All of this happened within such a short period of time that it was more than I could handle. I stayed so high the next week that I don't remember anything. My parents didn't want me to leave for Argentina before the celebration of Pops' life because we had always been so close, so I stayed around for that. They told me later that I was crying so hard at the funeral that my dad had to carry me out. I was doing whatever I could to kill the pain with drugs, but I didn't forget what I had promised to do.

My dad told me he was going to be the one to take me to Argentina, and Gerks took me shopping to get clothes sometime before Pops' funeral. At this point, I was thinking maybe I'd give it a shot for ten days and then, if it didn't help (which I was pretty sure it wouldn't),

I'd come back. Mom and Dad said they would take that; they just wanted me to give it a try. There was the question of whether the police were going to put out a warrant for my arrest in Brian's death, so my dad called again to make sure no warrant had been issued. It hadn't. Everything seemed clear for me to go.

The night before we left, I drove around looking for a dealer so I could get a last shot of heroin and also stock up on enough methadone to get me down to Argentina. I wanted a head start because I knew the place in Argentina wasn't like the first rehab I went to. It was all natural and didn't use any drugs. Methadone makes you high for about forty-eight hours, but it's a "replacement" drug that keeps you from using because it blocks the high you get from heroin. It's a kind of high, but not the same thing, and it helps you not be dope sick from withdrawal. I got a lot—two bottles. The dealer, a different one from my normal dealer, made me have sex with him in the car in exchange for the drugs.

The next day, my dad and I were on our way to the airport.

Do You Need Immediate Help?

For Immediate help,
call the 988 Suicide and Crisis Lifeline,
available 24/7.
https://988lifeline.org/media-resources/
"If you or someone you know is experiencing a mental health or
substance use crisis, call or text 988"

chapter

7

Finding Myself in Unfamiliar Places

I was super-nervous to be going to another country.

I was also very nervous about being dope sick because the treatment center doesn't use any medicine. They use traditional medicine and what they call "practical philosophy" to help you change the way you see life and develop new ways of thinking. So I knew there would be no methadone, no Suboxone, none of the stuff I'd had before to help with withdrawal symptoms and adjusting to being off of heroin. The idea of being dope sick for days was frightening to me, and I was kind of skeptical about how this would work. But I knew I had to try for Pops. I had promised, so I was going to do it.

We'd been through some really difficult times in the last few weeks, but there were still some funny things that happened on our trip. I remember my dad asking me a million times if I'd put drugs in his bags. "Just tell me if they're there," he kept saying. "I just need to know before we go through security."

"I told you, I didn't put anything in your bag," I said. I had to say it again and again.

Of course there weren't any drugs—not in his bag, anyway. I had the last bottle of methadone in my bag, and I went to the bathroom at the airport to take it. I also had been drinking a little bit, so I was really out of it. One of my dad's favorite stories to tell from our trip is how I asked him on the plane if we were going to see the Great Wall of China while we were flying to Argentina. He was so embarrassed that I didn't even know where I was going.

When we arrived in Buenos Aires, two guys from CMI Abasto, the treatment center, were there to pick me up. They were both named George, but one was called Crabby to distinguish them. Crabby was one of the philosophy coaches, and he ended up being like a grandfather figure to me. He reminded me so much of my grandpa that I started calling him that. He loved to cook and was full of life, joking around and saying funny things all the time. During my time there, we went to his house for parties and cookouts. I spent a lot of time with him. He was like my grandpa throughout my whole treatment.

I was amazed when I got to the treatment center. I walked into a gated building that opened up into a courtyard. From there, you can see ivy on the walls and rooms with a balcony, and it's absolutely beautiful. We walked through the courtyard and then were taken right into the dining room, and there was so much food laid out that it looked like a king's table. Everybody started yelling, "Hi, how are you?" just as if they were old friends. They hugged me and kissed me and were so happy and full of joy. *Oh my God,* I thought, *these people cannot actually be this happy.* I'd never experienced anything like it.

This big welcome was an introduction to one of CMI's main philosophies: enjoying life and experiencing true pleasure as an alternative to the destructive highs of drugs. The whole idea is to do everything with pleasure rather than punishment and pain. So they have this huge celebration with tons of food and start treating you as part of their loving family right away. They do it for everyone—patients, clients, visitors—and it can be overwhelming. It really does make you feel welcome, and it breaks down your defenses immediately. I started to feel at home pretty quickly.

I was still kind of out of it, but I remember eating better than I had ever eaten. I met all the philosophy coaches and started getting to know the rest of the staff. I was still afraid of being dope sick, but there was a woman we called Mamacita who quickly became my everything. The first night, she made me what they called sleepy-time tea, and she sat there and rubbed my back and my feet all night because I was starting to feel sick.

When I woke up the next morning, the staff started me on a lot of testing—sleep tests, brain scans, ultrasounds, bloodwork, X-rays, a full workup right off the bat, much of which continued throughout the week. I was sure I was going to be so sick I couldn't handle it, but my dad and I actually went out shopping with one of the guys there after a day of testing and had lunch. That night, I went to dinner and didn't get sick. I was super-tired, but not dope sick, which I didn't even know was possible. Maybe part of it was that they were so welcoming that it calmed my nerves, but for whatever reason, I never felt too bad. It was pretty amazing to go through that without the expected pain and discomfort.

The whole week was mostly about getting oriented—me getting to know them, and them getting to know me. I went through a lot of tests and interviews, and we talked about my history and my thoughts on what I wanted out of the program. I was introduced to the entire staff of trainers, dieticians, pharmacists, therapists, psychologists, and the philosophy coaches who do most of the one-on-one work with clients. I began getting used to the environment and the people.

Some didn't speak any English, so trying to figure out how to communicate with them was interesting. One time I wanted eggs for breakfast, so I went down to the kitchen and tried to explain to the cook what I wanted. I started flapping my arms and trying to create a picture of an egg coming out from a chicken—it was pretty awkward and hilarious—and he just kind of stared at me. But he got the idea and made me some eggs. One of the nurses who would come to my room each night to take vital signs and give me my prescriptions would just start laughing when I tried to talk to her. She said "no" to everything, even though she didn't understand me and I didn't understand her, but she still laughed whenever she came to my room. Trying to communicate made for a lot of funny situations.

My dad and I became extremely close that first week. He went out for coffee with a couple of the center's leaders one day, so he had a chance to give his perspective on the last few years, and they could see the pain he had been carrying and how exhausted he was. We had tons of conversations while he was there about everything we had both been through. I was able to get really honest about what my life looked like and told him how sorry I was, and we said a lot of things that started to heal some of the damage that had been done in our relationship over the previous few years.

Hearing Dad's heartache through this whole time was really hard. He was a police officer, so he knew what was involved in the life I was living. He saw it up close all the time. My parents continually thought they were going to lose me, and there were times I'd almost died. He told me how they felt like they were always just waiting for a phone call, afraid for where I was, wondering what I was doing. I know it was all so hard on them. Dad told me he loved me no matter what and that he was proud of me for taking the step to come to Argentina and finally get treatment. He just expressed how much he cared about me and how proud he was of me in general.

We did some fun things together too. He was staying in a hotel and came over every day to see me, and sometimes we'd go out to dinner. I had been kind of shocked that he was the one taking me there; he usually wasn't the one taking me to do things. I'd thought that maybe he was just over it in terms of my lifestyle. But I knew he didn't think I was beyond help or had ever lost faith in me. He was very much in favor of me coming, and even though he and Mom saw this as perhaps a last chance, they were hoping for the best. Now we were having an opportunity to get very close.

Dad called Mom often during the first few days at CMI, and he could tell right away that this was going to be a good situation for me. He told her that I was already being kinder in the way I spoke and seemed to have a clearer head. He already saw some pretty big changes.

True to my word, I gave rehab a try for ten days. That was all I had committed to. But I could tell by the end of ten days that this was going to help me, and I decided I wanted to stay. I wanted to become a different person, and I believed that the treatment center could help me figure out who I was and how to live differently. I was willing to commit to the process. So after the ten days, Dad told me again how proud he was that I went through with coming to Argentina and then left to go home.

You get a philosophy coach as soon as you get to CMI Abasto, and my coach and I did a lot together. We had one-on-one times but also group meetings where we talked about high and low feelings, determining where our emotions were at different times and how to manage them. CMI's basic approach is that you have to know yourself. That's the main issue behind addiction—that if you don't know yourself, you can't love yourself, and if you don't love yourself, you end up hurting yourself. People who become addicted to drugs want answers about who they really are, and when those answers are missing, they use drugs to create an excited feeling or numb themselves to their pain. So you have to become an active observer of who you are, noticing your emotions and ideas, recognizing which ones are the true you and are good for you as opposed to those that will harm you. Instead of just putting a bandage on deep emotional or medical issues, you have to understand your own uniqueness. The coaches are there to help that whole process.

My coach would see things in me that I wasn't even aware of. It was amazing. And when something would happen that pointed to a harmful thought pattern—something that might get some kind of punishment in other situations—she would help me observe the pattern and figure out what thoughts might produce better outcomes. It was all about replacing old habits, or old conditioned responses, with new ones. The coaches are the main people who facilitate that, but then they talk with the whole team of doctors, psychologists, and everyone else who's there to help you with these changes. I began to recognize a lot of the issues and patterns that had led me down the wrong path to begin with and had kept me there.

Sometimes we watched movies or read books and wrote down the emotions we saw and felt, as well as anything else we picked up on in terms of philosophy toward life. It helps not only to observe yourself but to observe other people—you see things more objectively in other lives—so movies and books are great ways to see the "characters" you have within yourself, learn how they move and what effects they have, and then learn how to control them. We would observe high emotions or ideas and low emotions or ideas and recognize how they operate. I also liked to listen to music and find the highs and lows there too. Then sometimes we would apply it to basic life experiences, like going out to shop or get coffee, and then come back and go through what I was feeling and how I was responding to those experiences.

I put in a ton of work with my coaches—a lot of looking inside myself, learning to recognize and respond to emotional ups and downs, learning how the mind and body work and different ways to approach life. Learning how to journal about yourself objectively is a big part of the program, so I wrote in a journal every day, and then we'd talk about what I had written in one-on-one sessions with my coach.

There were a lot of black holes in my past in terms of what I could remember, mainly because of how high I was most of the time, but also because of some of the traumas I experienced. We had to try to relocate a lot of those memories because I had buried them. We worked on the real root of when my addiction started, what happened, what was behind it, and all of that. There were many aspects of life I had not paid attention to over the years because I was so focused on maintaining the habit. You get tunnel vision in that kind of lifestyle, even when so many other things are going on around you. They teach you how to experience life—how to live life every day without needing to be high. They taught me how to love life again.

It definitely wasn't easy. After about a month of being there, after days of some of the hardest work, I was ready to pack up and leave. I was done. My coach sat on my bed and helped me pack my suitcase. "I love you," she told me. "This is your decision."

As I was packing, I talked to her about all my emotions. I missed home, and even though I had promised Pops I would try this, it just wasn't working for me. I just didn't think I could do it.

"Okay. Are you ready?" she asked. We had been packing and talking for about an hour, and she had stayed calm the whole time.

"No. I want to stay," I told her.

So she helped me unpack everything. And that's what it was like there. They let you work through everything on your own. I felt so much love and compassion from them.

I stayed pretty aware of my feelings through all of this as we looked into my past. A ton of guilt for Brian's death came up. That was extremely hard to work through, and it took a while to learn to be at peace with it, at least in some sense. Not that I'll ever be completely at peace with it, but I learned how to cope with my feelings about it. I still feel guilty, of course; that is not something you ever really get over. But I wrote a letter to Brian while I was there, and we took that letter and some white flowers to a bridge and threw them in the water. It was symbolic of letting go of my guilt and closing the door with him, and it felt like a huge relief. I felt like he knew I loved him and was sorry, and I felt at peace.

I also learned how much self-hatred I had—how far back it went, how it affected the way I thought in so many ways. I had spent much of my life apologizing for things like they were my fault, even when they weren't. I constantly said I was sorry for even the littlest things, and I didn't even know this about myself until they helped me notice it. It's hard to change something you've thought or done for years, or what other people have told you for most of your life. If you've been told you're stupid, for example, it's really hard to overcome that. Self-perception has to change. But it can happen, and it did in a pretty short period of time.

I came to understand how self-hatred had negatively shaped so much of my life. It would have changed many of my relationships, especially the guys I dated. I wouldn't have needed their attention so desperately, and I wouldn't have stayed with them when they began saying hurtful things to me. If I had been confident in myself and believed in my abilities, I think medical assistant school would have been different. I would have been able to get a good job and keep it. If I hadn't had that self-hatred, my whole life would have been different.

I had to learn to love and forgive myself. I went through a process of forgiving everyone and wrote in my journal about it. I forgave Shane, the boyfriend who first gave me heroin, for example. I forgave him for going to prison and making me feel like I was alone in the world. I wrote a letter explaining my feelings and telling him that I was forgiving him and letting it go. But I also wrote a letter to myself, forgiving myself for all the things I had done and letting it all go. I had to learn to accept myself for who I am. The coaches helped me begin to love and respect myself, and that was a huge change in my thinking.

I learned how to enjoy life too. Life can be enjoyed without getting high. We played board games in the dining room, and I started dancing again, which I hadn't done since I was very young. I took dance classes with one of the men who taught there. He taught me to be a girl again—to walk and talk like a woman—and he did my hair and nails and helped me feel beautiful and not see myself as ugly anymore. Whenever we got together, I felt at peace and learned so much from him.

Sometimes staff would take us out to a club and have a couple of drinks, learning how to stop at just one or two and just enjoy that for what it was. So much of the treatment was about learning to laugh and have fun again—to experience life's pleasures in a healthy way—so outings might include things like bowling, theater, sports, or even opera.

Crabby, the George who became my "grandpa" throughout my treatment, took me out sometimes. We would do something special together every week—a lunch or dinner, or something fun that was just for me apart from the group. One of the things I had always enjoyed with Pops was cooking Thanksgiving dinner every year. I'd spend the night with him, and we'd cook for the whole family. So my Argentina grandpa started cooking with me too, and one time we cooked a Thanksgiving dinner for everyone, just like I had done with Pops. Even though Pops was no longer with us, it helped me feel close to him, and it helped me feel a special connection with Crabby.

Crabby was also an acrobatic pilot. He used to be one of the best in the world and is now an instructor. One time we were watching an airshow, and I made a comment about wanting to go up in the plane one day, even though I've always been terrified of flying. Without me knowing it, he and the CMI staff talked about whether I'd be able to handle that situation and whether it would be a good experience for me, and they decided it would. So for my birthday, he took me up in a two-seater plane, and I got to take the controls for a while. It was an amazing experience.

CMI takes a holistic approach to recovery, so there's a dietician who creates a custom diet for each person. Early on, that helps with cravings that are common during withdrawal (especially for sweets), but it also helps establish healthy eating habits. They use a lot of natural foods without preservatives, and meals are always fresh. Daily exercise is encouraged too—drug use does a lot of damage to muscles—so they provide a trainer and give patients a membership at a local gym. I started developing a healthy lifestyle and felt better than I had in years.

I found out that I love to paint. I started painting my emotions, whether they were good or bad, almost every day. It was a little different each day, but I found it very helpful to try to represent what I was feeling visually. Sometimes I would wake up and have an emotion right away, so some of my paintings were of my morning feelings. But I really just painted whenever I had time to do it. And it was interesting to notice how they changed over time. Many of my first paintings were dark and expressed low emotions, but they got brighter and expressed higher emotions the longer I had been there. As I realized who I could be and felt more hopeful about life, my high-emotion paintings increased.

Some of my first paintings had images made out of words, like a tree composed of low-emotion words like hate, regret, judgment, and things like that. One was just a tangle of dark colors, as though it was something I was trying to escape from. Another had a black cloud raining down negative-emotion words. In some, I was a delicate flower, and the flower was often trying to grow even with adversity going on around it. One of my first paintings had a flower with petals falling off of it and bandage on the stem. The words above it said, "Being healed," because that's what I was doing there—growing back into what I needed to be. A later painting showed flower stems in a dark pot, then a flower halfway grown, and then a full, beautiful flower—a picture of how all the ups and downs of life are part of growth. No one has a perfect life; everyone has ups and downs. But those experiences are all part of learning and growing into something beautiful.

I also painted hearts—dark for hearts in trouble or pain, light for life and hope. One of my paintings pictured a black heart and another next to it that was pink with "life again" in blue letters. A split heart showed a low, dark side with the words, "You are nothing," and a pink, hopeful side.

I found that I loved to paint sunsets. They give me peace and calm, so whenever I wanted to represent positive, high-emotion thoughts, I would do it with a sunset. One of my paintings pictured a dove flying into the beautiful colors of a sunset at the end of my cure.

I saw myself as a dove, having life again and doing the things I needed to do—to be a better Brittany and a better mom than I was before.

I made a box to hold some of my things, and I painted a word on each side of the box and on each side of its lid. Every morning when I woke up, I would see words that reminded me of who I am, encourage me to stay focused on healing, and help me keep going—words like warrior, faith, thanks, love, wisdom, believe, joy, and hope. On the top of the box I wrote "cure," and I put a mirror on the lid so I could see myself next to that word. Every time I opened that box, I saw myself and thought: *Gotta keep going.*

One of our coaches gave us a project to gather all our tasks so we could show the work we had done. I made two book folders: one of all my work and my tools for getting my cure, which had every single task, every movie, every assignment they had given us. On the back I wrote: "Never give up." The second book was on how things had changed for me and with my family, my coaches, and all my other relationships. Even though I was working on myself and feeling good, I still needed to remember the past and know how things had changed. On the back of that book I wrote: "RIP 2 the girl I used 2 be! Her days are over! New day to come!" I was filling my life with a new identity—with hope, promise, and the constant awareness that things would be different from now on. I wasn't just hoping for a cure. I was on my way to it.

My whole year of being an inpatient was a good balance of philosophy sessions and life activities. I'd get my hair done sometimes, they gave massages and chiropractic treatment once a week, and we went to the gym every day. Because working on yourself can be very intense, we sometimes did something called "sleep therapy;" from Friday night to Monday morning, we stayed in our rooms to rest our brains, maybe watch some movies, and just relax. They brought food in and gave us relaxants to make us sleepy so we could just rest the whole two days. It was a nice break from all the emotional work during the weeks.

I kept using the tools the coaches were giving me, and the way I looked at life changed. I changed physically too. I worked out a lot and was getting in shape. I realized how much more I was enjoying life than I ever had. I was surrounded by people who cared about me and loved me, and we became like a family. That doesn't happen on the streets. You need people there, but you end up using them because everyone is just trying to get what they need for themselves. Here it was great to see how much people loved and cared.

Most of my friends at CMI Abasto were from Holland, Michigan, and they all had the same reason for being there. It isn't that our community was prone to drug use more than any other, but even communities with strong values can have problems like this. I'm not sure why so many from the same town found their way to the same rehab place in Argentina; maybe after one or two found help there, word of mouth persuaded other people to go too or gave them the idea or connections to try it out. I also know that there are some generous people in our town who were willing to fund rehab for these people, which may not happen in every community. But being around people I knew from home made me still feel very connected. All the guys from Holland thought of me as their little sister. We weren't all there at exactly the same time, but we overlapped enough that I became really close with several of them. The friend whose family first recommended CMI to my parents was still there when I arrived, and we became great friends. He was there for me every step of the way and played a big part in saving my life.

It didn't take long for my family to start noticing some big changes in my life. I talked with them online often. They got to know most of the staff there through Skype calls, and they noticed how well I got along with everybody. They could see that I was thinking more clearly and more positively, that I wasn't angry like I had been, that I could laugh more easily, that I looked healthier, and that I was getting a lot of my self-confidence back that I had had as a child.

My mom got to see this in person when she came to visit for my birthday after I was there for a few months. We went shopping and went out to eat a lot. The staff showed her everything I was working on, and she got to ask a lot of questions and see how their approach was working. She could tell I was learning a lot of tools for how to handle emotions and recognize my responses to certain situations. She saw a huge difference in my self-esteem, and we were able to just relax and have a great time.

After I had been an inpatient about a year, I went into outpatient treatment. That meant living in an apartment just down the road from the center. I lived on the top floor and could come and go on my own. Sometimes I'd go shopping or out to eat, but I still liked to go to the center for lunch or dinner or movies—I was still really involved with the activities there—and of course was still going to coaching sessions. I had a schedule of going to the gym, getting massages, and seeing the doctors. Sometimes I'd go back for sleep therapy too. I also worked even more closely with my coach as an outpatient. She would come to my apartment, and we'd go through my journal and dive into the feelings I'd been having that week. We'd talk about what I saw myself doing in the future some too, but we really focused on how I felt and how I was dealing with those feelings.

I realized at some point that through this whole experience, I never once felt like I wanted to turn back to heroin. That was not my experience in my first rehab, where I constantly wanted to get out and use again. After about two months at CMI Abasto, I never had another urge or need for drugs, not even in dreams or wandering thoughts. I went through some hard times there—days when I wished I could go home and see my family rather than just have video calls with them—but I never had the craving to get high. I could tell something had changed in me, that I had turned a corner in life.

When things were going well in Argentina, I got in touch with Amanda to try to get her to come down too. I would even help with fundraising for her if I could. We had talked several times about what coming to Argentina would look like for her, and I think she was thinking about it. I was excited about being with her again.

A few days later, I heard that Amanda had passed away from an overdose. Once again, I had to work through some feelings of guilt. I felt like I'd let another person down—that I had essentially killed another person because I couldn't act quickly enough. I knew that wasn't true. I hadn't actually had anything to do with Amanda's death. But I wished I had done more to get her there and had tried sooner.

There were other things happening back home too. My brother got married to the girlfriend he had been with since high school. I was excited that she was now my sister-in-law. We had gotten close over the years. She came over sometimes when I was living with my parents, and when my brother was living with my parents, I'd go see them and she and I would hang out. There were times when I was bouncing around from place to place that she'd have me spend some nights with her, and it was nice just to have a girls' night. I'd bring some drinks over, we'd hang out, and I felt very safe and welcomed. It was good to know that she was in the family.

My brother had been going to school to be a police officer like my dad, and I think my experiences shaped how they saw their jobs. My dad later told me that he sometimes took food to hookers on the street because he could see a little of me in them—girls who had had a lot of bad breaks and gotten in over their heads. Whenever he had to arrest someone for possession, he didn't really want to do it because instead of seeing their guilt he saw their struggles based on what I had gone through. My dad and brother had a lot of compassion for many of the people they had to deal with every day.

As for me, I was getting used to living in another country and being at least in some sense on my own. I learned a lot of Spanish so I could get by. Every three months, I had to take a boat across the Rio de la Plata to Uruguay to get my visa renewed, and I have a lot of good memories about those trips. I usually went with my Mamacita and some of the guys who were also in treatment, and we'd have lunch, walk around, get some coffee, and just enjoy the day. Usually we were there just for a few hours, but one time we got to go to a soccer game. I had never seen anything like that. There was so much energy, and we had so much fun because it was such a different experience for us. I was enjoying life in ways I never had, and I realized I was learning a lot about myself—things I wish I had known many years before—and feeling a sense of accomplishment.

I was proud of myself, excited about my future, and hopeful that maybe I was going to have a normal life that I had been wishing for and fighting to have for so long. I felt inner peace for maybe the first time in my life. If someone had asked me what the likelihood of going back to drugs was, I would have confidently told them it was zero. I was over the hump. I was learning a new way to live.

Do You Need Immediate Help?

For Immediate help,
call the 988 Suicide and Crisis Lifeline,
available 24/7.
https://988lifeline.org/media-resources/
"If you or someone you know is experiencing a mental health or substance use crisis, call or text 988"

Learning to Love Again

I was learning a lot of new life skills—embracing new ways of thinking about myself and other people, being able to have fun without feeling like I needed to get high, facing and letting go of a lot of the pain of my past, and even just getting used to a new lifestyle. But there was still something else I needed to learn to do in new ways: dating.

I was able to date as an outpatient, but my Mamacita would always have to go with me the first time I went out with someone. It was a little awkward telling a guy I could go out with him but my mama had to come with me. But most of the time I told them why and prepared them for what it would be like, so they usually didn't say much about it.

One time I wanted to go out with a guy who made my best friend very uneasy, so I had to bring two guys and Mama with me. They all sat in a booth behind me, and as it turns out, they were right about their suspicions. I'm glad they came with me because it wasn't a good date. But most of the time, especially if I felt comfortable about going out with someone, only Mama would come.

I started talking to one guy online, and I really wanted to get to know him better. His name was Matty, he was very cute and very nice, and he seemed different from anyone else I had dated. I started to build up some hope that this might work out. Mama decided it would be okay for us to go out for coffee, and of course she would come with me. She had just bought me a little key chain with a monkey on it named Bananas, so we decided that would be our code word if she approved of him.

I wanted to make a good impression and wore a black dress, and right away at the coffee shop we seemed to hit it off. Everything felt very natural. It was going really well. Matty was so sweet and funny, and I could tell Mama was really loving him. She somehow worked bananas into our conversation—almost just blurted it out, and it was really awkward. She definitely approved.

I always had to tell a date about my past the first time we went out. I explained that I was in treatment and laid out what my life looked like before. I never got too nervous about that. I figured that this was my story, and if a guy didn't like it, then he was someone I couldn't be with. But I was surprised whenever someone was okay with it.

Matty handled it really well. He said he was actually proud of me for what I was doing and thankful that I was getting help. That was a good sign. As we were leaving, Mama gave us some privacy, and he asked me out again. I had to go across the river to Uruguay the next day to renew my visa, but we went out for dinner and a movie after I got back. He was my total opposite in a lot of ways—he had never smoked a cigarette or taken a drink and was super-educated. He had a warm heart that just opened up to anyone. I could tell he was very compassionate and enjoyed life. I was hooked.

We talked about random things on our second date. I told him about the soccer game I'd gone to not long before and what that was like for me as someone who had never experienced that. We talked about my short trip to Uruguay that I had just come back from. When you lead off a first date with the kind of story I had, every conversation becomes easy. So we had a great time talking and getting to know each other. It was one of the best nights I ever had.

After that second date, we were never apart. He moved in with me not long afterward because I was close to the bank where he worked. We just didn't want to be away from each other. The people at CMI Abasto were very supportive. My coach at the time loved him, and we involved him in some coaching at times too. We became very close—friends, lovers, everything. And we did everything together. I didn't have much money, so when I was planning to move to another apartment, the manager of my building told me I could move to a smaller unit downstairs that wasn't as expensive. Matty and I had only a twin bed, so that's what we slept on. The apartment was infested with roaches—there are lots of them in Argentina—and it was just a horrible living situation. But we embraced it. I was so happy that it didn't matter where I was. We got through it together. I was full of joy.

I went to meet his mom one night, and she heard my story too. I felt absolutely no judgment from her. She embraced me right away. Eventually we moved in with her. His mom is an amazing woman, and I never felt any judgment from her or anyone in his family. That was surprising to me because I had almost always experienced judgment from people. Addicts know that even when people are trying not to judge, there always seems to be a little bit of judgment there anyway. But Matty's family didn't give me that sense at all. His mom wanted to hear my story. Neither she nor I slept very well, so sometimes I'd go downstairs in the middle of the night and find her there, and we'd have coffee and talk. She saw right away that I loved her son. We'd cook dinners together while Matty was at work, and I thought she just was a ball of fun.

I met Matty's dad and grandmother too; he had never brought anyone home to meet his father, who was separated from Matty's mom. I was super-nervous to meet them for the first time, but it was great. Again, I felt pure compassion and open arms. His brother lived with us for a little while, and he was the same way. The whole family was very accepting. They all tried to speak to me with the English they knew, and I tried to learn more and more Spanish to speak with them. We got to know each other really well.

Matty would go to work during the days, and I mostly stayed at home with his mom. I learned to cook a lot of new things with her. Sometimes I would go to the center and help out with new patients, and when Matty was home, we'd go for long walks. Buenos Aires is a beautiful city with so much to do, and I was falling deeply in love. I knew there was no one else for me, and he felt the same way. So after my second year of being there, I decided to continue with outpatient treatment.

I continued to Skype with my family three or four times a week. They were different conversations than I had ever had with them. I could tell that the way I talked with my family, especially my dad, was better than before. The dynamics had changed, which was noticeable early on, even from long distance, but especially when my mom came to down to see me for my birthday. My uncle came down for a visit too. So there had been plenty of communication, and they were up-to-date with everything I was doing, including my relationship with

Matty. They met him in our online conversations and got to know him pretty well from a distance.

My parents had never thought highly of my choice of boyfriends, or in the case of Brian, with the timing of the relationship. But they had seen changes in me in my time in Argentina, and they could tell I was making healthier decisions. They saw that I was able to create some boundaries for myself that I thought were good for me at CMI even in situations where I was allowed to have more freedom. So this time, they weren't worried that I might be making a bad decision.

They also liked Matty. He was funny, they could tell he was nice to me and cared for me, and he didn't even drink or smoke. Over time, as we talked to them online, they saw us enjoying life together, even laughing when difficult things were going on, like not having water at our apartment or dealing with the power going out. They could tell this was different and that my attitude toward life and other people had changed. They were comfortable with our relationship.

They did wonder what that relationship might mean for the long term. Would I choose to stay in Argentina? Would he follow me if I came home? And after Matty and I had been together for about a year, we were asking the same questions. We started talking about me going home again.

There were several factors involved with that. One was that my parents could no longer fund me in Argentina. At one point when I was an outpatient, I started doing some fundraising to be able to stay there longer because I didn't feel like I was ready to leave treatment. A lot of encouraging changes happened in the first few months of treatment, and sometimes it looks like the treatment has already done its work, but it takes much longer for those new habits and thought patterns to become conditioned reflexes.

It's like learning to drive. At first you have to think about everything, and only over time do all the decisions related to driving become automatic. I had learned a lot and made some pretty big changes, but I was still thinking about them rather than living with automatic reflexes. So I felt like I needed more time. I called potential donors back in Michigan, including Jeff Elhart from the car dealership, since he knew my grandparents and a little bit about my situation. I was able to extend my stay. But I knew I wouldn't be able to extend it indefinitely.

I also wanted to see my daughter and the rest of my family, and I knew I eventually needed to take care of the legal issues back home so I could travel back and forth. Other than my dad the first week, my mom visiting on one of my birthdays, and my uncle visiting during my time as outpatient, I hadn't seen anyone from home in three years. I wanted to go back.

Matty was fine with that. We talked about what that would look like for us as a couple. We figured he would come with me sometimes, and I'd go back to stay in Argentina sometimes. We weren't sure about anything permanent with the way visas worked. Like every girl, I probably dreamed about marriage one day, but that wasn't really on my radar yet, and probably wasn't on his radar either. But we were just going to try to make it work for now, and we knew we could figure out something going back and forth. I knew in the back of my mind that there was a possibility of losing him if I went home—that there was a chance he might not come, or that we'd lose interest in going back and forth over time—and I was nervous about that. I was also nervous about being home again after nearly three years. I had a lot of emotions about the whole idea, but I felt like it was something I needed to do.

I eventually decided just to do it. I called the authorities in Michigan and told them I was coming home.

This had been an ongoing issue with my parents, even from the start. While my dad was with me that first week in Argentina, a member of the U.S. Marshals kept calling my mom and threatening to arrest my dad for taking me out of the country. She was at home alone with three kids—Alison and two foster boys—and having to deal with the idea that Dad might lose his job. She kept telling this marshal that there was not a warrant out for my arrest when I left, which was true, but he kept calling me a fugitive and threatening to have Dad arrested. She didn't tell him any of that when he was with me in Argentina, but when Dad got home, he told the marshal to get his story straight with the detective who was saying there was a warrant when there wasn't. They actually had to prove that no warrant existed.

Still, the marshal called him from time to time while I was in Argentina to ask if I had come back and to make sure they would let him know ahead of time whenever I did.

So I knew to call ahead, and I wanted to deal with whatever legal matters were still up in the air. The Oakland County authorities asked me when I was coming, I gave them the date, and they told me to come in the morning after I arrived and turn myself in. I knew on the flight that I'd have to deal with that the next day, and since I'm terrified of flying anyway, it was not a pleasant trip. I took some medicine and had a couple drinks to help me relax on the plane, but there was also the uncertainty of stepping back into that old environment again. I knew it would be great to see my family, and I knew I had to report to the authorities, but I didn't know what else to expect.

Do You Need Immediate Help?

For Immediate help,
call the 988 Suicide and Crisis Lifeline,
available 24/7.
https://988lifeline.org/media-resources/
"If you or someone you know is experiencing a mental health or
substance use crisis, call or text 988"

My Return

When the plane finally landed Atlanta and I got off, U.S. Marshals were there to meet me and placed me under arrest for possession. That's not what I had been told on the phone, so I was completely taken by surprise. My heart sank.

They had a very old picture of me from when I was on drugs and I had sores all over my face, and when they showed it to me, I had a flashback of that life. I couldn't believe that's who I was. I thought, *I'm not that girl anymore.*

They took me to some kind of holding cell in the airport, searched all of my bags, and then walked me to the next plane. They never did ask me anything. They just said that I had a warrant out for my arrest, that I needed to get on the next plane, and that officers would be there waiting for me as soon as I got off.

I called my parents and told them what was happening, and they started making their way to the airport to be there when I arrived. When I landed in Grand Rapids, I went through being arrested all over again. My parents only got to hug me very briefly and then watch me being handcuffed and taken away. I was with them two minutes after being away for two-and-a-half years. And all I could think was how much this sucked.

I was taken directly to the county jail after I landed. There wasn't a way to call my parents yet and let them know where I was. They didn't know if I was going somewhere local or directly to Oakland County in Detroit, where my warrant came from, so for a while, they had no idea where I would be.

While I was being held in the county jail, a female officer pulled me aside and gave me some encouragement.

"You look like you're doing really well," she said. "Oakland County jail is a rough place, so here's what you need to do."

She gave me some advice about how to handle myself and told me I would be there through the weekend. "This is Friday, and no one gets out on the weekend, so you won't see a judge until Monday. But don't worry, everything will be okay."

That was nice of her to encourage me, but I was so frustrated that I was going to have to spend the weekend in jail. I called my parents and told them what she had said, and after a while the Oakland County officers came and picked me up. So after three years of being far removed from this life, I was put in a maximum-security holding cell in Detroit right before the weekend. I couldn't see the judge until Monday, so I would have to stay for three nights.

I hardly ate or drank anything at all those days. We were let out of our cell for an hour a day, so that's the only break I got. I was alone most of the time, and I was terrified.

It seemed like I was face-to-face with my whole past again, and all the old triggers were right there to confront me. I called my parents several times, very briefly, and told them how scared I was. It was a rough place to be.

I still thought coming back was the right decision; I don't remember wishing I had just stayed in Argentina. But the idea of being locked up after having been completely out of that lifestyle for years was depressing. I felt like I would have to develop that tough, hardened personality again. And I envisioned things just going downhill—having to do jail time, being around people with problems I had gotten away from, and missing out on a lot of the things I hoped would happen when I got back home.

But even in that environment, I never felt the urge to do drugs again. Even with all the old triggers around me, I still felt like there was zero chance I'd go back to that.

I settled in my mind that if this was what I had to do to get to the next stage of living my life, then this is just what I would do. Matty was constantly calling my parents for updates, and my brother was trying to get information from within the system. I could talk to my parents for ten minutes a day, but otherwise it was a miserable time, and I just wanted it to be over.

On Monday, I went in front of the judge on the computer, and he told me I was released until my next hearing.

I was so excited when my name was called and I was released. I didn't know if anyone would be there to meet me, but I just wanted out. I put on my shoes without even tying the laces, grabbed all my stuff as quickly as I could, and walked outside. I didn't really know where I was or if I'd see anyone I knew, but I was so relieved to get out of there that I didn't care if I had to walk around looking for some way to call my parents. I just wanted out as soon as possible.

Mom and Dad had already come. Nobody had been in touch with them to tell them exactly what was going on, so they brought money because they didn't know if they would have to pay any bail for me to get out.

First they pulled up to a side door at the county jail and were told that we had to go to the courthouse. They didn't know yet that my meeting with the judge was a video call. So they were trying to figure out where to go and what to do. All of a sudden, the door where they had parked opened up, and I walked out. They were shocked to see me, and I was so happy to see them. They kept asking me if they needed to pay somewhere or if I needed to check in with anyone, and I didn't know. I just told them they let me out, and here I was.

After a time of trying to figure out what to do—my dad was astonished that they let someone out of jail to walk around without papers or bail or any other formalities—we were told to go to another town for all that. They took my passport there and gave me a court date.

My return home had gotten off to a rocky start, but at least I was home.

I knew I would be given a court-appointed lawyer, but there was no contact ahead of my court date, and I didn't know what to expect. Even though it wasn't likely, I was terrified that I was going to have to do some time because I was looking at possession of heroin, morphine, and marijuana in the aftermath of Brian's death. Mom took me to court when it was time—I'm not sure why we didn't bring Dad, since he had worked in the system for so long and had a much better idea of how these things worked—but we figured it would mostly be a formality and I'd end up with probation.

When we finally did see my court-appointed attorney, he only talked with us for a couple of minutes. He agreed that this was just a matter of procedure, and since I had been clean for more than two years, the judge would put me on probation for a while. But the whole atmosphere was very intimidating. Most of the people who were there for their court appearances looked really rough and were in chains. I definitely didn't fit in.

When I finally got called to the stand, I heard the other lawyer say they wanted to charge me also with cause of death. My heart sank. Mom was crying. I was so scared, my hands got sweaty, and I turned pale.

The lawyers and the judge talked for a while—it seemed like a really long time—and I started to imagine all the horrible things they might say when they were done.

I just couldn't go to prison. I wasn't afraid of wanting drugs again, but I couldn't bear the thought of going back into that world of dealers and users.

Then the judge suddenly cut the conversation off and spoke. She pointed out that I had already done nearly three years of treatment and said words I'll never forget: "I believe she can do this. I believe one can make it through our system."

Then she ordered me to be released on probation for a year.

I cannot describe the relief I felt when I heard her say those words. I couldn't believe it. I was so excited that I was only going on probation and wouldn't have to do jail time. My mom and I went out for lunch and celebrated.

The first place I stayed after being released was with Gerks at her condo in an independent living place called Freedom Village. I can't imagine a better name considering what had happened in that court-room and what I had experienced over the last three years. I needed a job and a place to live, so we started looking for both right away. Just three days after I was released, I went to the Pizza Hut across the street from Freedom Village to pick up pizza for us, and I saw that they were hiring. I met the manager, asked for an application, and she talked to me for a little while and offered me a job on the spot.

Matty was coming in just a couple of weeks, so I found a place for us to live soon after starting work. I didn't have a probation officer yet, but the way the system worked was that I got a color assigned to me, and I had to call in every morning before 6 a.m. to see if my color was called for that day. If it was, I had to go in for a drug and alcohol screening. I basically had to be ready to pee for the judicial system every day for a year, which could be really inconvenient. But I never had to worry about anything being detected. My manager at Pizza Hut was very understanding about the whole process—she played a big role in my sobriety and helping me while I was figuring life out.

When Matty came back, we moved into our new apartment. We didn't have everything planned out. All I knew before returning was that I would come home, deal with the legal consequences of what had happened before I went to Argentina, and wait for him to come a few weeks later. That's all we were able to plan. He didn't have a work visa, so we knew he wouldn't be able to get a job right away. But we knew we would figure it out as we went along.

Matty had already met my family through all those Skype calls when I was in Argentina, so he had gotten to know my parents and my daughter well. We had actually all grown pretty close.

What I didn't know was that soon after Matty arrived, he had talked with my parents alone and asked their permission to marry me. He had it all set up. He had arranged to arrive in time for my birthday, so we made plans to celebrate, and I thought that was all it was going to be—a birthday celebration. He took me out to a mall and bought me tons of stuff. I looked like one of those girls in the movies loaded down with a bunch of shopping bags. And then he took me to dinner at one of my favorite Italian restaurants that had also been one of Pops' favorites too. He completely spoiled me.

I was totally surprised when Matty asked me to marry him. Caught completely off guard. I hadn't picked up on any hints that a proposal was coming, but I didn't even have to think about it. Hell yes! I knew he was the man for me.

For the first time, I couldn't believe how well my life was going. I also couldn't believe how much Matty reminded me of my Pops. He made me laugh with little jokes just like Pops always did, and he had the same big heart Pops always seemed to have. He seemed like the kind of guy who could fulfill that dream of having a relationship like the one my grandparents had. I knew Pops would have loved him if they had met.

We got married after a couple of months in a very down-to-earth ceremony because we didn't have much money and had to put it together quickly, before Matty's visa lapsed and he would have to go back to Argentina. We hired a lawyer—we had been saving and had set some money aside before coming back to the U.S.—and he walked us through all the steps for Matty to get his green card. My parents helped us pay for our wedding.

For about the first six months, Matty couldn't work. I was the only one earning an income, and it was hard to keep up with payments on our apartment, so we moved back in with my grandma at Freedom Village for a while.

By this time, I had been assigned a probation officer, who was very helpful and helped me get through everything. She believed in me and was really amazing. She didn't feel like she was just doing a job; she actually cared and talked with me to see how I was doing. But once when we were at Freedom Village, there was some kind of mix-up, and another probation officer came to visit and asked at the office where I lived. In that conversation, it slipped that I was on probation. We were asked to leave the complex.

We didn't know where to go at first. We lived out of our car for a few days. My parents now had five foster kids. Their heart for helping people had just kept growing, which was a great thing to see, but it meant that living with them long-term wasn't an option. But they had the attitude of this is something that needed to be done, so we'd figure it out.

We went and stayed with them for a little while because we had nowhere else to go. They also had a friend who said we could live at their place, but only after their college-age child went back to school after a few weeks. They had a nice basement apartment with a full kitchen and a separate garage. We spent several months not being in the same place for very long, moving back and forth, nothing set in stone, and everything feeling so uncertain. But we were in love, and we knew we would figure everything out as we went along.

I continued to work at Pizza Hut until Matty was able to get a work visa and get a job in banking after about a year. But during all this time, even being back in my home state and around all of the old triggers from my past, and even while we were going through some difficult challenges in our living situation, I never felt tempted to turn back to heroin. I wanted my life to be different now. My family supported me 100 percent, I had a new husband, and I wanted to do well for my daughter. And I knew I could. I knew there was something better at the end of all this.

After we had been in the basement apartment of my parents' friends for about three months, I started having really bad pains in my stomach. I felt extremely sick. I couldn't keep any food down, and I was losing weight. One night, I couldn't take it anymore and said I was going to go to the emergency room. Matty is suspicious of doctors and medicine, and he didn't think I should go. He wanted me to wait and see if it passed. But I was in so much pain that I felt like I had to go.

When I got to the hospital, they took me to an emergency room and did a lot of tests, including some ultrasounds. After a while, the doctor came in and said, "Well, you're pregnant."

"No, I'm not," I said. "I can't be." I sounded like my mother when she found out I was pregnant years before. Having a baby just wasn't part of our plan. We had moved around so much and were still trying to get our feet on the ground, and this wasn't in the cards. But there it was on the ultrasound picture—a little baby. I was in disbelief.

So was everyone else. I called Matty, and he said, "Oh my God, no you're not—you need to come home." I went home and showed him the pictures, and I was actually pretty far along, somewhere around two months. We called my parents, and they could hardly believe it too. But they were happy. And we were happy. We were just very surprised.

Matty had just started working at a bank when we found out I was pregnant. We were still living in the basement apartment and had no money yet. So we definitely felt a lot of nerves about this. My parents were great; they said we'd all just figure it out as we went and that they were there for us. But our whole future suddenly looked different.

My pregnancy did not go very well. It was really rough. I stayed violently sick the whole time, and I ended up on bedrest for much of it because I kept going into labor. Certain smells would trigger nausea and vomiting, which made work very difficult. I never felt well the whole time.

Once we knew the gender, we had a gender-reveal party. My family has not had a boy in nearly 30 years. My brother had one girl (he has three now), and of course my first child was a girl. So no one felt very surprised when we found out this one was going to be a girl too, but we were all still very excited about another one coming into the family.

Seven months into my pregnancy, I had a baby shower. The night before, I hadn't felt her moving, so I was a little concerned. I wasn't hungry at my party, but that wasn't especially unusual considering how bad I felt so much of the time. It also didn't seem unusual that I kept leaking and thinking I was peeing because that happened often too. But when we took a break from opening presents, I went in the back room and talked to my mom.

"How do you know if your water breaks?" I asked.

"Your water didn't break," she said. "You would know if you did because it would be all over the floor. You're fine. We need to get back out there and open the rest of your presents."

"Okay," I said. "I'm just having some more contractions." Peeing and having contractions had become kind of normal for me.

So I went back and finished opening my presents, and as people were starting to leave, I turned to my mother and asked, "Do you have any underwear?"

She gave me a pair, and I leaked through those right away too. Then Matty showed up after a run; we were about to go to a baseball game with people from his work that night. I was already looking forward to my cheese dog and cheese fries. Mom met him at the door, and after he found out what was happening, he surprisingly suggested that we go to the hospital.

I got to the hospital wearing my five-inch heels, said hello to everybody up front—they were used to me by now—and went upstairs to be examined. The doctor said he wanted to do a test to make sure I wasn't leaking amniotic fluid. His test showed that I had been. The doctor turned to Matty and asked if he was ready to have a baby in an hour, and Matty asked if he could shower first. That's all he could think of in that moment. So the doctor told him to make it fast, and he did. Then right away, they did an emergency C-section. My daughter came two months early.

I had been getting injections to help with her development, so even though Sarah was the smallest baby in the NICU, she was the healthiest. We had to tube-feed her for only two days.

We stayed in the hospital for a week because I was having some trouble. I was bleeding from the spinal tap, so they had to fuse my spine. The fuse didn't go as planned, and I got infected, so they called in a neurologist and bone specialist who poked and prodded at me so much that I kept crying. My husband put his arms around me at one point as I was crying and yelling and said, "Please don't touch her anymore! Just stop!" I felt so bad. I had a high fever and was in a lot of pain in addition to the pain from the C-section. And because I had a fever, I couldn't see Sarah. It was a horrible experience.

They finally got the infection under control, and I was able to see my daughter again. They sent us home at the same time, but we had nothing there we could use yet. We had some things from the baby shower, but she was too small for the car seat and the clothes we had for her, and we didn't have a crib yet. We were still living in the basement apartment, but we were also talking about getting our own place. We had been planning to look at apartments and move—we hoped before our daughter came—but we weren't able to do that when she arrived early. Now that she was here, we needed to find another place to live.

Now that Matty was working, we had enough money to move, and we found a two-bedroom apartment soon after Sarah was born. I physically wasn't able to work yet, but I had a job lined up too. While

I had been pregnant, Matty and I were shopping at a store downtown for shoes for him to wear to work, and we saw Jeff Elhart, who I had called from Argentina while I was raising funds for rehab, so he knew all about how things had gone for me in recent years and knew I had gotten the help I needed at the treatment center. We talked for a while, and Jeff offered to buy Matty's shoes, which meant the world to us. It was so encouraging that he wanted to help.

Jeff asked me to think about working for his dealership and to come into an interview sometime, whenever the time was right. Based on my fundraising call to him when I was in Argentina, he said he was impressed with how I communicate with people. So I went in later for an interview and got hired, even though I couldn't start working there until after Sarah came and I had recovered. It took so much pressure off us to know that this opportunity was out there waiting for me.

Meanwhile, I had a lot of ongoing medical issues. Matty didn't go with me to my four-week checkup after Sarah's birth because I thought it would be a normal doctor's appointment. But the doctor asked me if I wanted to have more children. I said yes, and he went on to explain that he didn't think it was a good idea. For one thing, Sarah had come very early and with a lot of complications for both of us, and he couldn't promise that I or my next child would be safe through another childbirth. If I did get pregnant, he said, I would need to be on injections and bedrest throughout the pregnancy.

I had not expected to hear that and was definitely taken aback. I was very confused at first, and I felt extremely sad, like something was being taken away from me. But Matty and I talked about the possibility of something happening to me in childbirth and him having two children to take care of without me there. We didn't want that. So because of the risks to me and our next child, we decided to have my tubes tied.

A couple of weeks later, the doctor did a relatively non-invasive procedure in which a coil is inserted into the tube, and the scar tissue that grows round it eventually blocks the tube. I went back in after a few months to make sure the tubes had closed, and when they injected the dye for the confirmation test, one of my tubes burst and I had to have an emergency hysterectomy.

I had a hard time with this because even though I knew I wasn't going to have any more children, removing my reproductive parts just seemed so final. I also knew the recovery was going to be difficult. Matty would have to take on a lot more caregiving for Sarah because I wouldn't be able to lift her for a while. We knew things were going to be tough for a few months.

After about six months, I was well enough to start work at Elhart Automotive. My first day on the job was Valentine's Day. I showed up for work, excited to start this new position, and fifteen minutes in, I got a call that Matty had been in a serious car accident. My manager told me to take the day off and go be with my husband. It turned out that Matty's car had flipped three times, and it was such a bad accident that the road had been shut down. One of my brother's friends had called him, since he was a police officer, to tell him about the accident and said, "Oh my God, I don't know if anyone is alive from this." He had no idea Matty was involved. But Matty miraculously walked away with only a Band-Aid on his hand. He was fine. I had envisioned working for a full day and then going home to have a TV dinner with the love of my life, so things hadn't gone exactly as I planned. But I was grateful that he was miraculously spared.

I loved being a mom again. This time I was very involved, of course. Sarah was an easy baby; she only woke up once a night. And just as I had felt with Alison years before, the feeling of taking care of this beautiful life was amazing. I knew she would be my last, so the desire to connect and be with her was strong. I was filled with love, peace, and enjoyment.

Do You Need Immediate Help?

*For Immediate help,
call the 988 Suicide and Crisis Lifeline,
available 24/7.
https://988lifeline.org/media-resources/
"If you or someone you know is experiencing a mental health or
substance use crisis, call or text 988"*

A New Self, a New Hope

I would love to say that life has been perfect since rehab. And it has been good. There's no doubt about that. Marriage, getting back on our feet with jobs and our living situation, and becoming a mom again are things worth celebrating. I am truly grateful to be living that "normal" life that I used to long for.

Actually, I don't believe anyone's life is normal. Every person's experience is different and unique to them. But the difference between my life on drugs and my life with a family, home, and career is amazing.

But it isn't perfect. There were times after Sarah's birth when Matty and I really struggled. Even though she was very healthy for a premature baby that first week, some complicating health issues developed, including a kidney infection that was kind of touch and go. That put a lot of stress on our marriage in terms of trying to manage everything. But there were also other stresses that started pulling us apart too. We didn't hang out or talk as much, and it seemed like we were falling out of love. Between his work, my work, his accident, and moving all the time from place to place, even living out of our car for a time, we had a lot going on and didn't feel like we had a firm foundation for dealing with it all.

I had learned a lot about myself in Argentina, but these were situations I didn't quite know how to respond to. I often reacted to Matty with a lot of anger. I exploded in every single argument we had. Sometimes I would storm out and go to a friend's house; my friend George was great about calming me down, talking me off the ledge, reminding me that going through difficulties and disagreements is part of all normal relationships, and that we could work things out. But sometimes I'd leave and not come back until 2 or 3 in the morning, and I started drinking more too. It wasn't a very productive way to respond.

I had met George several years before, and he became a close friend, not only to me but also to Matty. Sarah calls him Uncle George. He has always been extremely supportive and was kind of like a mediator, able to see my side and Matty's side of things. To this day, he comes over for cookouts and dinners and has been very involved in our lives for years. He's part of the family. There were times when Matty and I were on the edge of whether to stay married or not, and George really helped us through.

All of these challenges could have torn Matty and me apart if we let them, and we almost did. We got some marriage counseling, which really helped, and over time we began to fall in love with each other again. Part of what helped was being diagnosed with bipolar disorder. It has made a huge difference in how I see myself, and it makes me wonder what my life could have been like when I was younger if I had known about it. A lot of the ways I reacted to things at school, those mood swings in junior high and high school, all those emotional ups and downs I've always experienced, and a lot of the attitudes I had and decisions I made might have been handled differently if we had understood what was going on. But I'm glad to know now, and it has helped our marriage tremendously. Matty understands me a lot more too. Just knowing that is an issue has created a lot more understanding and improved our relationship.

It was difficult finding out about this diagnosis because there's a stigma that comes with it. People have a negative perception of bipolar people, and I didn't want to be thought of as a crazy person. That was one of the things that made me feel really down, and I struggled with it a lot at first. But understanding what it involves, that it means having extreme mood swings between emotional highs and lows—something I spent a lot of time working on in Argentina—it made sense to me. I've probably had this my whole life, and knowing about it when I was younger would have saved me from trying to self-medicate. Apparently, I was always trying to run away and protect myself from the pain I felt. Since the diagnosis, I've gotten my medication under control, I've had fewer outbursts and arguments, and I understand myself better.

Through all of this, there have been times when self-hatred started to creep back in. I've wondered if I was being a good wife or mother—that feeling of not being enough, or a sense of being alone even when I had a lot of people around me. I've really struggled at times with some of my old insecurities.

Many experiences since coming back from Argentina could have brought me back down or pulled me back into the old temptations to seek relief. The good news is that they haven't. I've had a lot of ups and downs that would have caused many former addicts to cave and go get high again, but I haven't once thought that I wanted to turn back to that. Even being around some of the kinds of things that used to be triggers for me, I still have not felt any urge to return to drugs. When I was in the hospital for Sarah's birth, I was given pain medication—something doctors are always extremely careful about with former addicts because it might provoke the addiction again. But for me, it didn't provoke any urges, conditioned reflexes, feelings of dependency on it, or anything else. My time in Argentina had dealt with the root issue so thoroughly that even using pain medication had no effect on my desire to have it again.

Sarah is strong, sassy, and independent, but she has continued to have some medical issues—five surgeries for various problems. But she's doing great and is a handful, just like I was. Alison is in high school now, and she and I see each other all the time now. She still lives with my parents, but sometimes she spends the night with us, and sometimes Sarah goes over to my parents to spend the night with them. The girls love each other and get along great. Alison knows her mom made a lot of wrong decisions, and that I ultimately had to go away in order to fix myself. She still calls me mom, and she knows I tried and unfortunately couldn't be there for her. But we have a great relationship now. I am trying to be there for her as much as I can.

My relationships with family members today are good. I'm very close to my family now, and we do everything together. Things couldn't be better with my mom and dad. They are always there for me and my family. We often go a cottage in the summer to fish and go tubing. Mom always puts together a Christmas trip for the family, and it's always so much fun. My brother and I are still close, and I am very close to my sister-in-law too. We have four girls between us who are near to each other in age, so we are busy all the time. We have lots of family get-togethers.

Needless to say, I have my whole family back, and they have me back. They finally get to see the new Brittany. Love was always there, but any trust and happiness that had been lost have been restored now too. I love feeling this way about my whole family again. Years ago, I don't know if I could have foreseen growing as a family with my brother and sister-in-law or having Alison back in my life as much as she is. She is growing up to be an amazing girl.

Gerks died not long after I moved back from Argentina, but both sets of my grandparents in Chicago are still around, although Papa and Nana live in Florida much of the time. They enjoy golf and stay active, and Matty and I try to go see them when we can. They love Sarah and spoil her. I still talk to GG often—I call her every few days, we talk about every little thing, and we are very close. I see my her as much as I can too. She still sews and is always sending my kids clothes she made for them. She even makes clothes for Sarah's doll that match the ones she made for Sarah.

I also enjoy seeing Aunt Jodi, who now lives in Traverse City, and Aunt Ashley, who is still in Chicago. I stay in touch with my family as much as I can and am so glad for the relationships we have.

Jeff, my employer, has become something of a grandfather figure to me, which means a lot since he knew Pops and I already associated him with that relationship. He has almost filled the void that Pops left in my life. Jeff hired me based on my communication skills that he experienced when I called him from Argentina, so he started me at his dealership's call center, where I would call past customers to check on how satisfied they were with their purchase or see if they were in the market for a new or used car. I had no idea I was good at that kind of thing, but apparently I was. I'm grateful Jeff was able to recognize that and gave me the opportunity to work for him.

At the time I'm writing this, I've been clean for ten years, and I have no doubt that will continue. Life isn't easy, and I don't think anyone would look at my life and say it's perfectly happy without any bumps in the road. But it's enjoyable. I still have to figure out who I am and what that looks like, and being able to balance work, life, and everything else feels like an everyday struggle sometimes. I still believe you have to keep your head down, keep going, never stop believing in yourself, and trust that every step you take is for a reason. That's what I try to do.

But when I look back over my life, I feel proud and inspired. I will never refer to myself as an addict—that is no longer my identity. It describes what I went through, but it does not describe who I am. I have learned to see myself as a new person, and I want other people to see me that way too.

I still wrestle with guilt and regret at times. I think that's normal, and I write down my thoughts about guilt and regret when they come up because I'm still dealing with the emotions that come with them. Learning to forgive myself was not just a one-time thing; it's ongoing, every single day. But I also have to keep my eye on my new life. It's something I've earned and deserve, and I'm not going to lose it. Even though I'm still processing the past, my focus is on living life now and in the future.

I believe there's a message in my story for anyone. Obviously, for people in addiction, I want them to feel understood and know that there's hope. It is possible to make it out of that life. That statistics are not good; almost all the friends I had in that life have either died or are in prison. The friend whose family told my family about CMI Abasto and how it had helped their son once said that eight of his ten friends that he had in that life were now dead, and two were in prison. That's true for me too; almost everyone I know from that time in my life is dead or locked up. Shane, the boyfriend who got me into it all was in rehab a few years ago, but that's the last I heard of him. I don't know how he did with that. Most people in that world have tragically died or are living a tragic life. And the longer someone stays in it, the more likely they are to lose their life or freedom.

I almost did several times. I once died and had to be shocked back to life. I almost died several other times, sometimes in trying to take my own life and other times by overdosing or being pulled into dangerous situations. I also could have easily ended up in prison on many occasions. Prison and/or death is what happened to many of the people I used to hang out with, and I'm always aware that those outcomes could have been my story too.

But no one needs to end up as a tragic statistic. The real tragedy is that the numbers don't have to be the way they are. You don't have to end up either dead or locked up. There's a third option. I'm an example of that, and there are others who can tell a similar story.

As it turns out, I'm the first woman to have made it all the way through CMI Abasto's treatment program. Nearly everyone who makes it through ends up remaining drug-free—they have more than a 99 percent success rate for those who complete in- and outpatient terms—but not everyone makes it through. Like I almost did, some pack up and leave when the hard work of learning about yourself feels too heavy. But for those who stick it out, the results are great.

So I hope my story is encouraging for those who struggle with addiction. But I believe it is also a message of hope and understanding for the families and friends of people trapped in addiction. It's important to realize how much pain and guilt an addicted person is going through, and that they may want to be a part of your family but don't feel like they can. Sometimes, as with me, there are mental health issues involved as well. It isn't as easy as just making a decision to get out of that life and come home. They are feeling shame, embarrassment, hopelessness, guilt, and so much more, and no matter how much they might want to come home, doing so requires facing those feelings. It's so much easier to keep trying to escape them, even though escaping them with another high will just stretch them out even longer. It hurts for friends and family members to see someone destroying their lives with addiction, but there is pain on both sides. The person struggling with addiction is hurting and doesn't know how to make the pain stop.

That's hard for families to understand, or to deal with even when they do understand it. Few families think this could happen to them. It isn't just kids who grow up in poor neighborhoods or without good parents. It happens in typical middle-class neighborhoods in families who give their kids a lot of love and care. What looks like a promising future can turn into a nightmare with a few bad influences or wrong decisions. It's important to prepare kids for the temptations out there and to know what to do when addiction seems to become a threat.

When it does become a part of a family's life, it's important to know what to do to be empathic without enabling, like my parents did. They had to learn how to say no, how to recognize attempts to manipulate or deceive, and how to be there in ways that would help without helping in ways that only fed the addiction. They had to put up with sleepless nights and unexpected phone calls, make a lot of hard decisions, and make every effort not to let an addiction tear their family apart. Seeking help from experienced people is vital for getting a family through something like this.

And most importantly, families of addicts need to hold onto hope. Nothing is impossible, even when it seems like an addict is too far gone or has resisted help for too long. My parents held onto faith and believed God had a plan and would make something good out of all they went through. Today, they can look back and see that as hard as it was, a lot of good things have come out of it.

In a more general sense, my story is a testimony of hope for any situation. Anyone caught in what seems like hopeless circumstances needs to know that there is always a way out. It may not be easy, but there's always hope for redemption and restoration. One of the paintings I did in Argentina showed a dark sky filled with stars, saying "even in darkness, we can find light." Both are parts of life, and even if you feel surrounded by darkness, that doesn't mean there isn't light somewhere. Sometimes it just takes time to find it.

Even for those who have not struggled with addiction or know someone who has, there are plenty of ways to help. People in treatment programs need funding, and even though some people say that giving money to help drug addicts is a waste of money, it isn't. I understand that attitude because a lot of people who have gone through some sort of treatment program have ended up returning to their drugs. But some programs can be very effective, and sometimes it takes more than one attempt for a user to break their habit. Families can't always fund that process, but outside support makes it possible for many people who would otherwise not be able to get help.

My parents are a great example of turning a crisis into an opportunity as they have now fostered several children of addicts who had no one to care for them. That's one way to help, but there are many others. Community programs that address addiction always welcome advocates and volunteers.

When I look ahead to the future, I feel hopeful. I see happiness, and I feel loved. I'm still open-minded with regard to my ups and downs, because I know those will always be a part of life. But I feel so much inspiration, passion, and love. I look forward to what's ahead. I have a lot of things to be grateful for, and a lot of hope that, long ago, didn't even seem possible.

Do You Need Immediate Help?

For Immediate help,
call the 988 Suicide and Crisis Lifeline,
available 24/7.
https://988lifeline.org/media-resources/
"If you or someone you know is experiencing a mental health or
substance use crisis, call or text 988"

The Takeaway

There is a way out. It starts with education.

I am a believer. Had I known what I know today, I wouldn't have found myself nearly dead on several occasions during my life. The following pages are added to my story so that you can help your loved ones avoid the mistakes that I experienced in my life. And even if someone is spiraling out of control, it's not too late! I am living proof of that!

Please allow me to introduce you to a special friend of mine. I referred to Jeff Elhart in my story earlier. Not only is Jeff someone who I really appreciate and came to my rescue when I needed it most, but he has a story to share with you that will change your life and potentially save the lives of those you love.

Following is an excerpt from the groundbreaking book [be nice. logo] – 4 SIMPLE STEPS To Recognize Depression and Prevent Suicide

What leads to suicide?

Brittany nearly died by suicide as a result of her struggles with her addiction to heroin. And, you'll recall that Brittany didn't suddenly just start using heroin—most users start with lesser drugs and become lured into harder drugs—which then leads to suicide contemplation. There are four major contributing factors that increase the chances of people dying by suicide (risk factors):

- Mental illness, (mostly depression) and other mental health disorders
- Substance abuse; alcohol, and narcotics
- Sexual abuse
- Domestic violence

Brittany experienced all of these—along with her drug addiction, a mental health disorder including depression, sexual abuse from her drug dealers, and domestic violence from her struggles in her drug-house experiences. Many situations like hers are high-risk for suicide.

There's no single cause for suicide. Suicide most often occurs when stressors and health issues converge to create an experience of hopelessness and despair. However, among the many contributors to the risk of suicide, and perhaps the four most prominent, are typically depression (and mental illness), substance abuse, domestic violence, and sexual abuse.

Mental Illness: Depression

Depression is the most common condition associated with suicide, and it is often undiagnosed or untreated. Conditions like depression, anxiety, and substance problems, especially when unaddressed, increase risk for suicide. Yet it's important to note that most people who actively manage their mental health conditions go on to engage in life in a positive manner. (American Federation for Suicide Prevention—AFSP)

Depression and suicide are linked, with an estimate that up to 60% of people who die by suicide have major depression. But it's important to note that this figure doesn't mean most people with depression will attempt suicide.

Research suggests that the majority of suicides are related to a psychiatric condition, including depression, substance use disorders, and psychosis. (verywellmind.com)

Substance Abuse

It is essential to understand the connection between suicide, depression, and substance abuse. Although not all individuals who experience depression have thoughts of suicide, depression is the leading cause of suicide. In 2014, about 60% of people who died by suicide suffered from a mood disorder, including major depression, bipolar disorder, and dysthymia. Many young people who kill themselves are both depressed and suffer from a substance abuse disorder. A 2018 survey revealed that substance abuse was more common for adolescents and adults who suffered from mental health issues than those who did not. Many people who experience mood disorders will seek out drugs and alcohol to self-medicate and alleviate negative feelings. Heavy use of drugs and alcohol has the potential to turn into a substance use disorder, which may increase the severity of a depressive episode, thus increasing the likelihood of suicide. It is also important to understand that depression symptoms may appear during early recovery from drugs and alcohol and can interfere with someone's recovery process. If the individual is not properly treated for depression, they may experience suicidal thoughts and may even attempt suicide. It is crucial for someone with substance abuse issues and depressive tendencies to find a treatment option that will focus on both issues.

Even if someone is experiencing a substance use disorder and thoughts of suicide, the result of suicide is not inevitable. Family and friends of someone with suicidal thoughts and substance abuse issues should begin an open, honest, and non-judgmental conversation with them.

Domestic Violence

Studies show that survivors of domestic violence, including dating violence, have higher-than-average rates of suicidal thoughts, with as many as 23 percent of survivors having attempted suicide compared to 3 percent among those who have not experienced domestic violence.

This includes not only exposure to repeated physical or sexual abuse, but also exposure to psychological or emotional abuse. Such abuse may cause victims to experience depression, hopelessness, and other forms of psychological distress.

Reasons for this correlation are complex and variable, but almost certainly include the severe and sustained stress that goes hand in hand with experiencing abuse, often encompassing humiliation, being controlled, isolation, and lack of access to money or other basic resources.

If an individual at risk for suicide because of interpersonal violence does not receive help, the risk of suicide may not abate even after the abuse ends. But there are things we can do increase safety from suicide among those who have experienced and are experiencing abuse. (Mental Health Association—MHA)

Some survivors may come forward with information about violence, but they may not mention the suicide ideation that accompanies it. Other survivors may talk about or even attempt suicide, but might not connect their feelings of hopelessness with abuse. This is why it's so important to recognize the link between domestic violence and suicide, and to ask clearly and directly about both risks. This can be done anywhere these concerns arise, whether at an emergency room, on a crisis line, in a doctor's office, or simply during a conversation with a friend or neighbor. Once the topic is bridged, strategies for coping, safety, and positive changes can be discussed.

If you encounter such a situation, some things you can do that can help are the following:

Call the National Suicide Prevention Lifeline at 988 or text them at 741-741. Or, call the Domestic Violence Hotline at 1-800-799-SAFE (7233).

Sexual Abuse

In 2020, a study investigated the relationship between suicide attempts and a history of sexual abuse. In a sample of 158 female suicide attempters aged 20 years or older, 50% of the subjects reported having been sexually abused at some time. Sexually abused suicide attempters had shown more suicidal behavior in the past than their non-sexually abused counterparts (even though they were significantly younger) and were characterized by a more severe problem history. In the past, as well as shortly after the index attempt, they had experienced more serious problems in their relationships with significant others, with sexuality, and with self-fulfillment. At follow-up one year later, significantly more sexually abused women had attempted suicide during the intervening period than the women without a history of sexual abuse, and they also had more serious sexual problems. It is concluded that within a group of female suicide attempters, those with a history of sexual abuse are disproportionately vulnerable to repeated suicidal behavior. (NIH)

As one of the top leading causes of death in the United States, particularly among young people, suicide can be considered one of the country's most significant health epidemics. It is the 10th leading cause of death among all age groups in the United States and is the second leading cause of death among people aged 10-34. In 2021, almost 50,000 Americans died of suicide, with approximately one suicide every 12 minutes, and 1.3 million American adults attempted suicide.

Those with alcohol dependence are ten times more likely than the general population to take their lives, and those who use drugs are 14 times more likely to do so. Additionally, 22% of suicidal deaths involved alcohol intoxication, 20% involved opiates, 10.2% involved marijuana, 4.6% involved cocaine, and 3.4% involved amphetamines.

According to multiple studies, over 50% of suicides are associated with dependence on drugs and alcohol, and at least 25% of people with alcohol or drug addiction die by committing suicide. Additionally, more than 70% of adolescent suicides are associated with drug and alcohol use and dependence.

Takeaway

Please read on. You will be introduced to and empowered by a simple, effective "toolbox" for helping those in your life who may be suffering with one of the risk factors mentioned above. These terrible illnesses and addictions are treatable. Suicide is preventable. You can get help for yourself or others, and you can help share this good news to many other people who desperately need it.

Do You Need Immediate Help?

For Immediate help,
call the 988 Suicide and Crisis Lifeline,
available 24/7.
https://988lifeline.org/media-resources/
"If you or someone you know is experiencing a mental health or substance use crisis, call or text 988"

Acknowledgements

I am grateful to Jeff Elhart, who has been a great friend since I was young, Jeff has been a great champion during my recovery stages and has provided encouragement and support for me to share my story through this book.

Chip Brown, my agent at Proper Media, has my gratitude for bringing this project to fruition and providing his expertise for me to portray my story in this publication.

To my Grandparents, parents and brother, a big part of why I have a story of hope to share, thank you for your unconditional love and support. I could not have done this without you, my pillars, who have never abandoned me and have always pushed me to get better.

Last but not least, to my Husband and Daughters, who have never judged me for my past or the mistakes I made. Your love and support have helped me grow into the woman I have always wanted to be.

To all of you who are a part of my life and story, I am here, stronger and happier than evr before. Thank you.

About the Author

I was born into a midwestern'values, conservative christian family. Our home was full of unconditional love and security. I loved being a big sister to my little brother and I was very close to my grandpapa and grandmama. But my dad and I had some hard times getting along—we would butt heads a lot.

In middle school, I started hanging out with people my parents considered "the wrong crowd," and I started acting up a lot and fighting with my mom and dad more. I began lying about my where-abouts and started doing poorly in school. I began to dislike myself. I never felt good enough for anyone. School was really hard for me because I had a learning disability, which lowered my self-esteem. I began dating a boy in high school and ended up getting pregnant when I was 16 which made school even harder for me. I broke up with my boyfriend after my daughter was born, and it devastated me. I was so in love with him. I dated another boy but he went to college after high school and I found myself alone with my daughter. It felt like my whole word ended. I decided to go to medical assistant school. I finally had a fresh start and a purpose.

However, this is where my life took a turn for the worst. I ended up hanging out with the wrong people. I was heavily drinking all the time and I began dating a guy with a friend group that was into drugs. Responding to pain I had from endometriosis, my boyfriend introduced me to hero-in—I was hooked immediately. I started doing whatever I need to in order to get my next fix. I was stealing and ended up living in a drug house.

My boyfriend and I would live without food and toilet paper in order to fund our drug habit. My boyfriend eventually had a warrant out for his arrest, and after much discussion, we decided he should turn himself in. This broke my heart, but we felt it was the right thing to do. As I saw my life by this point, this was just another person who left my life. However, this led me to go to rehab. I was there a few mouths, met another guy there and we got married. We quickly both got back into using drugs. I was in very deep right away. One fateful morning, I woke up and found my husband lying dead next to me in bed.

For a fresh start, I went to Chicago to stay with my grandparents. This was perfect because my grandpapa was like a father to me, but it turned out he was very sick with cancer and he died a few days after I got there. My life felt like it was coming to a end, so I attempted suicide, but I remembered that right before my grandpapa died, he asked me to go get help and I promised him I would. I went to a treatment center in Argentina for three years, using traditional medicine and philosophy. While in outpatient treatment in Argentina, I met a guy—We did everything together from day one. We went back to my hometown in Michigan together but upon my airplane landing, I was met by U.S. Marshalls and was sent directly to jail. This was hard for me and my family, but when I got out of jail, my parents were right there for me. My boyfriend from Argentia came to visit for my birthday and he asked me to marry him. I was pregnant again and was our family's financial provider, working at Pizza Hut. My baby was born two months early and I was put on bedrest. My husband became our financial provider at this point. When I recovered from my pregnancy, and my baby was healthy, I ultimately got a steady job at the successful

Elhart auto-dealership in my hometown where the owner Jeff Elhart became like a grandfather for me. My husband and I now both have solid jobs and although life has not been easy at all, and continues to have its ups and downs, we are very happy. I am living with my loving family who has always been here for me in all of this and loved me no matter what. I am now living what most call a normal and happy life. I am now happy. I am now normal. I am happy living my happy, normal life.

INTRODUCTION TO be nice.

4 SIMPLE STEPS to
Recognize Depression and Prevent Suicide

Shared by co-authors Christy Buck and Jeff Elhart:

So, how can you help someone who may be struggling—perhaps even silently—with any of these potentially deadly experiences?

It all starts with education, as Brittany mentioned. Without the proper understanding of what to look for in your loved ones, coworkers, friends, or even acquaintances, your task of helping them is difficult and even next to impossible. With proper education you will have the confidence to take action to help others receive the professional help they need.

The education tool backed by science and has equipped hundreds of thousands of people, perhaps like yourself, who are concerned about a loved one or friend who may be struggling with an addiction, mental illness, domestic violence, or even sexual abuse is called **be nice.**

The action plan **be nice.** is not a phrase to simply be nice to people, rather it is a simple action plan for all people to use to help improve and potentially save lives.

At its most basic, **be nice.** is an acrostic—a four-step action plan to notice, invite, challenge, and empower people to take action when they or someone they know may be experiencing the effects of depression, a substance abuse including liquor and drugs, domestic violence, and sexual abuse. Liken it to the simple steps of the common "Stop, Drop, and Roll" action plan to save oneself from a house fire. More specifically in practical terms, here is how to utilize the simplest means of recognizing the warning signs of depression, addiction, or abuse:

- **Notice** what is right so you can notice what is different in someone's moods or behavior.

- **Invite** yourself to reach out and have a caring conversation with that person.

- **Challenge** stigma by exploring why this person is exhibiting these changes, and challenge yourself to ask an important, direct question in a mental health crisis.

- **Empower** with resources and knowledge of next steps to get help. Stay by their side and assist when appropriate. That may mean connecting them with professional help—a counselor, psychologist, emergency room, or primary care physician. It might include a call to the 24-hour national suicide hotline at 988 or a text of "HOME" to 741741.

After reading **be nice. —4 SIMPLE STEPS to Recognize Depression and Prevent Suicide**, you will be armed with the knowledge to help others improve and even save their lives. Mental illness is treatable, and suicide is preventable. And you are part of the solution. You can help. Put **be nice.** into action.

Meet the Authors of *be nice.*

Christy Buck, LBSW
Executive Director
Mental Health Foundation of
West Michigan

Jeff Elhart
Playground Director II
Elhart Automotive Campus

The **be nice.** program and its action plan were created under Christy Buck's leadership by the Mental Health Foundation (MHF) in 2010. In 2015, the trajectory of the **be nice.** program changed the day the Elhart family reached out. Jeff Elhart called the MHF office in search of a resource at a mental health event he was hosting.

Since June 2015, together Christy and Jeff have worked tirelessly to impact a community by educating people of all genders, races, and socioeconomic classes on mental illness awareness and suicide prevention. Christy's trademarked **be nice.** program and Jeff's personal ambition to bring about change in this growing epidemic of depression and suicide has made a very passionate and ambitious pair in equipping communities with a culture that can improve and even save lives through a simple action plan . . . **be nice.**

Alongside of Christy and Jeff is an army of warriors helping to win this battle. The staff of Christy's organization, volunteers, and the community supporters for both foundations; the Mental Health Foundation of West Michigan; and the Wayne Elhart **be nice.** Memorial Fund have made a significant positive culture around this topic, reduced stigma, and equipped people to administer the "stop, drop, and roll" for those with mental illness and suicidal ideation.

This book shares the many years of professional experience in this field by Christy and the firsthand experience of a suicide loss survivor in Jeff.

MHF programs provide continuous education of mental illness awareness and suicide prevention education to almost 150,000 K-12 students each year throughout Michigan with the near-term strategic goal of making its scientific, evidence-based programming available nationally by 2024. The **be nice.** program is embraced not only by school students, parents, teachers, counselors, and administration but also small-to-large companies and houses of worship. Christy serves as a trustee on the Grandville Public School Board; is recognized as a leader in the community for mental health, suicide prevention, and stigma reduction; and has served on many task forces and committees.

Within her Holy Trinity Greek Orthodox Church community, she has served as the youth advisor and instructed Religious Education for more than thirty years.

Jeff Elhart has worked in the automobile business his entire career since the age of twelve. Along with his brother Wayne and father Kenneth, they successfully served the West Michigan community in offering sales and service of cars and trucks at their automobile dealerships. Having received many business and community recognition awards, the Elhart Automotive Campus continues serving its community under Jeff's leadership since his father's retirement in 1990 and his brother's retirement in 2010.

Since his brother's death from depression by suicide on March 27, 2015, he has become an advocate for mental illness awareness and suicide prevention. Jeff is a trained educational liaison for the Mental Health Foundation of West Michigan's **be nice.** program and has served on the MHF board as chairman and current board member. His company supports the MHF's mission and was the first business to implement the **be nice.** program. Jeff serves on the executive committee of the National Action Alliance for Suicide Prevention and serves on two task force committees: the Faith Community Task Force and the Workplace Task Force. He has served in numerous leadership positions in his Christian life by serving the churches where he has been a member. Jeff frequently speaks on the topic of mental illness awareness and suicide prevention in his industry of the automobile business as well as other organizations—including faith communities and others.

A Sneak Peek
Into
be nice.

Be nice. – 4 SIMPLE STEPS to Recognize Depression and Prevent Suicide

Meet Wayne Elhart

This man was successful, funny, and a joy to know.

It's hard to imagine that anyone would take their own life.

If you wonder,

Why would this man take his own life?,

YOU ARE NOT ALONE.

The truth is, suicide is reality for many people—people

you may know.

And . . . the pain and grief of those who are left behind is devastating.

This book is dedicated to the memory of Wayne Jeffery Elhart and others who

have died by suicide.

May your reading provide you the tools to

HELP OTHERS WITH MENTAL ILLNESS AND PREVENT SUICIDE.

Preface

Written by Wayne Elhart

Kathy, family & friends

I love you all.

This depression has gotten the best of me.

Do not blame yourself as it was me.

Please use my illness to help others ~~in my~~

God please help me to help others.

Wayne

PART ONE

Do not blame Yourself as it was me.

Recognizing Risks,
Seeing the Signs,
Saving Lives

Written by Jeff Elhart

You are about to read an account of Wayne's journey with depression. This story or a story like it may be totally foreign to you. If so, that's good news. It may, however, sound familiar to some of you as you may have experienced a similar tragedy in your personal life. Either way, I am sharing Wayne's story as it provides a roadmap of how many of us who struggle with a mental illness, mostly depression, can face dire thoughts and even take unbelievable action up to and including suicide. This book will provide you an action plan in just four simple steps to help others win the fight against this growing epidemic of depression and suicide.

Who Would Have Known?

Written by Jeff Elhart

It was the summer of 2010 when my cell phone registered an unexpected text message: "I love you."

My brother was fifty-six at the time. Not knowing how to deal with his message, I meditated on it for the day. My mind was churning. Was it sent by him? Was he just saying thank-you for my attempt to help him in his struggling time? Or did this mean Wayne was saying goodbye?

Playground Director

Sometime during the late 1990s, Wayne created new titles for his staff and himself. Everyone at Elhart Pontiac GMC Jeep, Inc. carried the title of CEO—Customer Relations. He gave himself the title of Playground Director.

Before his retirement in 2010, Wayne and I were partners in our family business, Elhart Automotive Campus in Holland, Michigan. The business, established in 1965 by our parents, Ken and Barbara Elhart, offers several brands: GMC Trucks, Nissan, Hyundai, Genesis, and Kia. We offered Pontiac, Jeep, and Dodge for most of those first fifty-five years, up to the time of the General Motors and Chrysler bankruptcy in 2009.

Wayne's directive to his staff was to treat the customer the way they would want to be treated. If they as a staff member had to make a decision to make sure that the customer experience was exceptional, then they were to do it. After all, they were the CEO of customer relations!

Being the Playground Director meant to Wayne that everyone at the dealership was there to work hard and play hard. If a situation came up on the playground of the dealership, Wayne would step in. That didn't happen often, but when it did, Wayne would use some directives after giving his playmates every opportunity to do the right thing. He might say, "This is my way or the highway," or, "Maybe you would be suited better somewhere else," or, "I didn't notice your name on the sign out front." Years later, even his terminated employees respected him for his forthrightness. Wayne didn't sugarcoat anything. You could take what he said to the bank.

You could count on Wayne. He provided the strength of leading from the top. He honored those who worked hard and rewarded them with opportunities to play hard. Through his ability to corral the troops on the playground, he was able to build and maintain a strong family atmosphere at work, at home, and with those he mentored.

Traveling the Road to the Bottom

Like the mountain passes in the Rockies, life's journey is not a straight or level road. That was the experience for most business owners and the American public during the financial recession of 2008 to 2010.

It was no different for Wayne, except he faced it head-on with the gifts God had given him. Wayne lived the fruit of the Spirit: love, joy, peace, forbearance, kindness, goodness, faithfulness, gentleness, and self-control. He used these gifts to lift the spirits of others around him—his family, his employees, his friends, and those he mentored. Despite Wayne's gift of sharing good cheer, he was not protected from hardship. The turmoil of the auto industry crisis in 2009 to 2010 created an environment he couldn't run from but had to face head-on. The journey of maneuvering through the bankruptcies of General Motors and Chrysler may have built character that Wayne already possessed, but it was the news of March 2010 that triggered his depression. As a result of the phone call from a General Motors executive, once a close business associate, the wind went out of Wayne's sails. The plans for our business under General Motors' reorganization took a 180-degree turn. Everything our family business had planned for was being overturned by the federal government.

If there was a tipping point in Wayne's life, this was it. Though he spoke with strength to his family, he was moving quickly into depression.

Noticeable Changes in Wayne

My wife, Cherie, and I took many walks down the Lake Michigan shoreline talking about Wayne during the early summer that year, 2010. We talked about Wayne's weight loss—thirty-plus pounds and noticeably leaner. We noticed his thinner face and gray complexion. I know his coworkers and friends noticed too.

Wayne was losing his positive attitude and outlook. He was having trouble making decisions and deferred many personnel decisions to me or at least asked what should be done. His normally confident nature was gone.

Wayne was drowning in his depression. It was fueled by fear of not being able to continue his family business and provide employment for his employees, many of whom had stood by him for decades. Wayne was a humble man who rarely expressed anger, but it still haunted him. He was angry at the government's interference with General Motors' reorganization plan. The sky was falling into his world. He wanted out.

My Own Journey with Depression

I had had my own bout with depression ten years earlier. It was triggered by guilt. In 2000, I released (okay, fired) a key employee who had worked with our family business for twenty-seven years. I've never been through a divorce, but that's the only way I can describe my pain at the time. Working with this employee, with all the successes and challenges we experienced together, was unforgettable. I couldn't just turn off the memories. My guilt turned into sadness. The good news is that I searched out a fix and learned that my sadness was depression.

When my doctor asked if anyone else in my family dealt with depression, I said my mother did. At the time, I didn't realize the degree with which she had been battling the illness so I didn't think much of it. I was just sad. I couldn't sleep. I couldn't get the guilt off my mind. A swirling feeling of downward pressure was new to me. My journey with depression lasted for several years, and the first was quite severe; I had to keep my mind occupied at all times or it would wander off to, "Why did I do that?" I beat myself up countless times and was losing my confidence at home and at work. The only person I told of my illness was Cherie. I hid it—or at least think I did—from everyone else. My doctor prescribed an antidepressant and told me it might take thirty-to-sixty days to feel the effect. Anxious and losing patience, I later called to see if a stronger dose would be acceptable. He doubled my dosage after about thirty days.

Time went on, and the hurt from the guilt continued. Between time and Zoloft, however, my mind was beginning to feel some ease from the constant pain. In about a year, I felt I was capable of living with the decision I had made, and it was time to slowly remove myself from the drug (with my doctor's assurance)—but I still held on to that nagging guilt.

Throwing Life-Rings

Having felt the effects of depression myself, I shared with Cherie that Wayne needed some help. I figured that if an antidepressant helped me, it could help him too. After all, we were brothers; we must have at least some of the same DNA. So one day in June 2010, I spoke to Wayne about seeing his doctor, who also happened to be mine. He said he would make the call to set up an appointment, but I sensed it was time to empower myself to make sure he did. I picked up the phone in his office, dialed our doctor, and handed the phone to Wayne. He made his appointment. Relieved that he was able to see the doctor that week, I felt we were one step closer to helping him overcome his depression.

The Text

That's when his text came. "I love you." Between June and July 2010, Wayne had isolated himself, lost his confidence and a lot of weight, felt hopeless and helpless and had difficulty getting out of bed. Sleeping through the night was not even in the picture. He was trying to hang on to a few life-rings thrown his way, but life was spiraling out of control.

Did the text mean he was thanking me for trying to help him? Or did it mean he was saying goodbye? I didn't know.

I also didn't know what to do with the text. Should I tell anyone about it? Was it real? Did it actually come from Wayne's fingers and from his phone?

I let it pass—for now.

A Time for Transition

The summer of 2010 goes down as a record of walks along the beach for Cherie and me. Dealing with our business turmoil and trying to help Wayne with his emotional strain, we leaned on God's beauty for motivation and discernment in our quest for solutions. Remembering that Wayne wanted to retire at fifty-five, Cherie suggested it might be a good time to consider the business transition, since Wayne was now fifty-six. We agreed to sleep on it.

I asked the question later that week. "Wayne, I know you wanted to retire at fifty-five. You're fifty-six now. Business is a challenge and not fun for you anymore. Is it time for our transition? I'd rather remain partners, but maybe it's worth considering."

I told him I wasn't sure if I had the funds to buy his half of the business, and he didn't know if he would have enough to live on in retirement. We decided to think about it for a couple of weeks, talk it over with our wives, and do due diligence with our attorney and accountant. During that time, I reached out to my uncle George, who had experience in the mental illness treatment industry. I told him what Wayne and I were considering, and George surprised me with his comments.

"I retired a few years ago, and I have to tell you my story. I was fine for about ninety days, but then I became bored with nothing to do. I felt worthless. I became depressed. I received some help and medication, and now I'm okay." But he went on to offer an important piece of advice to give to Wayne. "You have to make sure you have something to run to and not from when you choose to retire."

I thought that advice was perfect coming from a respected relative, so I asked George to meet with Wayne and his wife, Kathy, to have the same conversation. He agreed and talked with them the next week.

Wayne approached me in July and said he wanted to pursue the thought of the business transition. He was convinced he had enough to look forward to in retirement and felt ready for this change. But was he?

On the last day of 2010, Cherie and I purchased Wayne and Kathy's half of the business. And for the next three-and-a-half years until the summer of 2014, Wayne enjoyed life tremendously. He did the things he loved to do—skiing in the winter in Colorado and boating on Lake Michigan and Lake Huron during the summer. Wayne never saw a bluebird day in Colorado that he didn't ski at least twenty-five thousand vertical feet. One year he logged more than 1.3 million vertical feet over fifty-nine days! Later that summer, he traveled hundreds of miles and spent more than sixty days on our shared boat.

Wayne was a social butterfly. With his words, smile, and quick wit, he could bring an audience to their hands and knees, aching with laughter. He was a mentor to many, including those at our business and many other young men who are now successful businessmen in their respective fields. Many of them thought of Wayne as a second father.

But in 2014, he quit doing most of the things he enjoyed. He went the whole summer without putting his boat in the water. He didn't spend time on our family boat. He made no plans for skiing. He isolated himself again and was clearly depressed.

One September day, I asked Wayne how his summer had gone without boating. When he said one of his two dogs was sick and he felt he should stay home, I believed him. He and Kathy had no children, and I knew he cared a lot about those dogs. But I still knew he was depressed.

It was difficult to see, but I noticed that something more was needed than my shallow talks with him. Wayne's complexion was so white, and he looked so scared. I had Wayne call his doctor to set up an appointment for later that day. His doctor prescribed for him the same antidepressant that I was on. I thought that was the fix. In time, Wayne would be back to himself.

Just as I had been impatient with the results with my medication for depression, Wayne was feeling the same anxiety. His patience was running thin. He was getting thinner, now down forty pounds. Though

Wayne lived the fruit of the Spirit apart from attending a church, I knew medication of the brain was only one tool to help him. Another one would be faith.

It was just a few short months later that Cherie and I invited Wayne and Kathy to Florida to stay a few days with us. When in Florida, we attend Christ Fellowship, a large church in Palm Beach Gardens, so we all attended the weekend of December 7, 2014. The pastor spoke from Isaiah 43:2 (NIV): "When you pass through the waters, I will be with you; When you walk through the fire, you will not be burned; the flames will not set you ablaze." The pastor asked those who were struggling with inner demons to raise their hands and he would pray over them to receive Jesus as their Lord and Savior and ultimate healer of their troubles. Wayne's hand shot up like a rocket! The Holy Spirit was at work. Wayne received Jesus Christ as his Lord and Savior. He had been baptized in the Methodist Church as a youngster but did not have Jesus in his heart for decades and had not been involved in the church or spent time in the Bible. But from that day forward, Wayne was in the Word each and every day, seeking God's support for his struggles and looking for help in releasing the demons from his mind.

Just a few weeks later, Wayne said, "Jeff, look what I found!" He was holding a Bible. "Where did you find this?" I asked.

"Look inside the cover," he said.

I did. It was *The King James Version* of the Bible he received from our First United Methodist Church when he graduated from third grade Sunday School. "Wow, Wayne, that is so cool!"

"Yeah! I'm through Genesis already! There are a lot of thees and thous in there!"

His energy—and his sense of humor—seemed to be returning. While Wayne was showing some strength from his faith and medication, he was still distant from others and not like himself. I just so happened to be reading my favorite pastor Rick Warren's Daily Hope Devotional on January 19, 2015, when I thought I'd discovered the answer to Wayne's troubles. Rick spoke that day about "how to deal with how you feel." Rick Warren and his wife, Kay, became suicide loss survivors after they lost their son Matthew on April 6, 2013, at the age of twenty-seven to a lifelong illness of depression. Especially since their loss, Pastor Warren's messages frequently provide hope for those in our society who struggle with depression. Rick suggested that if you're struggling with your emotions, you're struggling with one of two emotions: worry/fear or anger. He suggested to determine which emotion it is, then define what you're afraid of or angry about. Then ask yourself if what you're feeling is true or not. I thought Wayne was dealing with fear, primarily that he would run out of money. So, I shared this devotional with him. I was right. He was afraid of running out of money. Were his perceptions right, or were those fears exaggerated—as fears often are? The best way to explore the truth of that fear was to have him meet with his accountant. He and Kathy did that a couple of weeks later, and it turned out that he was in great financial shape. He could put that fear behind him. I thought that was the fix.

It wasn't. It wasn't enough. I found Wayne dead on March 27, 2015.

Dying Wishes Granted

Written by Jeff Elhart

Wayne's battle with major depression had been relatively short, but it was much more intense than any of us knew. I and the rest of the family were shocked, and I wasn't sure what to do next or even what to think. Wayne and I had spent so much of life together—brothers, best friends, partners in business for more than three decades. I didn't know how to process what had happened. Once I got past the initial shock, the question of "why" kept coming up in my mind. And I didn't have any answers for it.

I had plenty of emotions, though. Survivors of suicide go through a wide range of feelings, and many experience anger or guilt, or a combination of the two. I knew I wasn't angry at Wayne, and I really didn't have any anger toward God for what had happened. But I experienced a lot of guilt. I had some deep battles with all the questions I had, particularly what I might have done differently to help Wayne before it was too late. How had I not noticed how much he was struggling? And if I had noticed, what would I have done? Why didn't I think to help him more than I did—to make sure everything was okay, even after his financial fears were settled? What else could I have done to prevent this horrible tragedy? I was glad I had done some things to help—I had gotten him to his primary care physician and helped him rediscover faith in God. But that hadn't been enough. At the time we had not found the note he had left behind to fill in any of the gaps for us. What had he been thinking? Why hadn't he reached out more? All these questions kept nagging at me, and they kept me up at night.

I Had to Come Up with a Fix

Because I felt such a sense of mission from Wayne's death, I dove into research. I consumed all kinds of books and resources about depression and suicide. I learned a lot, but nothing struck me as something I could use to equip everyday people in a meaningful way. But the underlying theme was consistent. Depression is not rocket science. Preventing suicide is not Superman work. Anybody and everybody can recognize the warning signs of depression and help the person get professional help or treatment before it's too late. But I quickly learned that it is up to the loved one, coworker, or anyone who connects with regularly with the person struggling with depression who needs to provide the help.

I decided to be very intentional about coming up with a fix. A few weeks after Wayne's death, Cherie and I went back to Florida to get away but most importantly visit the pastor who helped bring Wayne back into his relationship with God. The pastor said, "Oh my goodness, you need to come back to Christ Fellowship Church to see a new movie, *Hope Bridge*, we're showing! It's about depression and suicide. In fact, the movie producer was one of our worship leaders here not long ago. She and her husband now live in Cincinnati and have had an experience like yours. Come to the movie and meet them—David and Christie Eaton."

The movie, *Hope Bridge*, is about a high school boy who loses his father to suicide and goes on a mission to find out why. In his journey, he deals with anger, which grows to the point that he is ready to take his own life. After his counselor talks him off the ledge of a bridge, the counselor says, "It's not the pain that you're feeling. It's the fear of the pain that you're feeling."

At the end of the movie, the boy takes the reminders of his anger and burns them in his family's backyard. Then, with his mother and sister, he spreads those ashes around a new tree planted in the yard in his dad's memory.

This scene prompted me to take action with my guilt. I wrote down eleven specific situations in which, in my mind, I could have done something to help Wayne and did not. Two months after his death, we held a memorial service on Wayne's birthday by a flagpole on our dealership property. We buried part of Wayne's remains in an urn next to the flagpole. I wrote a letter to Wayne, attached the eleven situations, and inserted it into the urn. At that moment, I felt myself lifted off the ground with God's hands. I had been rid of 80 percent of the guilt I suffered with.

When we brought *Hope Bridge* to our church and community in Michigan, I invited about twenty organizations to participate by having a booth outside the sanctuary so they could provide resources on mental health, counseling, and more. I reached out to the Mental Health Foundation of West Michigan to participate and spoke to Christy Buck, whom I had never met before.

"I need to come out and meet you!" she said.

When we met for the first time, I told her I was looking for a simple tool to help people understand the warning signs of depression and how to help those who are depressed before a life is lost. I had been trying to come up with something with the word *depression* as an acronym. Cherie had told me, "You need something simple, like 'stop, drop, and roll.'" I knew she was right. When Christy told me about be nice., forming an acrostic with the word *nice*—**notice, invite, challenge, empower**—I knew that was it. I found the fix. "At its most basic," Christy said, "**be nice.** is a four-step action plan to notice, invite, challenge, and empower people to take action when they or someone they know may be experiencing a change in their mental health. Take it a step further and **be nice.** becomes an upstream program that uses the action plan as a basis for mental health and suicide prevention education in schools, workplaces, places of worship, and communities."

Yes, this was it! One of my biggest prayers in my life was answered on June 29, 2015, just ninety days after Wayne's death. I found the tool to help others with the illness of depression and a tool to educate people, all people, on how to save a life from suicide. **be nice.** is the "stop, drop, and roll" for mental illness awareness and suicide prevention education. Period.

The Letter and Confirmation

Sixteen months after Wayne's death, his wife, Kathy, hosted a small gathering of some of their closest friends. During the cookout, she started to feel cold and went inside to get a jacket from the closet.

One of Wayne's old windbreakers was still there. For some reason she had kept it on her side of their coat closet and grabbed it, though she'd never worn it before. She put it on and continued to enjoy the company. They reminisced about Wayne, and memories of the good times were starting to feel more natural.

Kathy reached into the jacket pocket—maybe for a tissue, maybe to warm her hands, or maybe just out of habit. She felt a piece of paper, pulled it out, unfolded it, and read the words written on it:

Kathy, family & friends,
I love you all.
This depression has gotten the best of me.
Do not blame yourself as it was me.
Please use my illness to help others.
God help me to help others.
Wayne

Our family received some sense of closure from Wayne through that letter. Since Wayne's death, my father had been suffering with silent anger, sometimes saying, "That rascal, why did he do that?"

When I showed him the letter, he said, "I'm proud of Wayne." It was closure for him. My mother said, "Oh, the pain he must have been in. He wrote this letter knowing you were going to find it, Jeff. He knew you would do something about it."

Wayne's request was already being answered months before we found his note. We were well on our way to providing mental illness awareness and suicide prevention education in our community and beyond. However, his letter made me feel like I needed to put things in overdrive. And we did.

Even though it was too late to save Wayne, I could honor the request he left in his last written words. He wanted his experience somehow to help others. Even in his last days, he reached out for us—not to help him, but to help other people going through what he had been going through. This became my mission.

Regardless of all the "ifs" that plagued me—what I might have been able to do for Wayne before he died—there was nothing I could do for him now. But I could honor that request. There were plenty of other people like him who needed help. I had been struggling so much with what else I could have done to help him, but I hadn't known how to recognize the warning signs that were there. And I wouldn't have known what to do even if I had noticed them. But what if we could prevent the same thing from happening to other families? What if there was a tool that could equip people to identify mental illness in others and then help them get the help they need? What if there was a way for people to know what to do? Those are the questions **be nice.** answered for us.

Looking Back—and Looking Ahead

As I mentioned, I have depression. I've taken medication for it since 2011. Major changes in my life triggered my depression, much as life events triggered Wayne's. I didn't consider suicide, although there were times when I would cry during the night wishing I could make the pain end. A cousin died from depression by suicide about thirty years ago, and I remember thinking then that suicide was a very selfish way to die. I had a friend who died by suicide about twelve years ago, and again I had the same feeling. Now I know better. It isn't a selfish act but a simple equation. Those who die by suicide feel that their pain exceeds the gain they think remains in their lives. In their mind, their pain is greater than their gain. Simply put, PAIN > GAIN.

Looking back, I can see how Wayne's pain became greater than his perceived gain. I can now also fit the warning signs into the **be nice.** action plan. I noticed the changes in his behavior after the life-altering event of a bankruptcy that disrupted his lifelong passion— the car business. I noticed his weight loss, his pale complexion, his inability to get out of bed in the morning, his loss of confidence, and so much more. I noticed that he didn't put his boat in the water all summer, that he quit doing a lot of things he loved to do, that he didn't make plans for his usual ski trip that fall, and that he quit enjoying a drink like he used to. He even texted, "I love you." I didn't pick up on that signal but wish I had.

I invited myself to initiate a conversation with Wayne in which I expressed concern about his change in behavior—especially the lack of boating and skiing. I showed love, respect, and concern for him because of these changes I was observing. But I wish I had known then   what I know now about taking the next steps. I accepted Wayne's answers about why he wasn't boating and skiing anymore without challenging him with the tough question: "Are you thinking of killing yourself?" I empowered him to see a doctor and get on an antidepressant, and I empowered him to go to church and read his Bible. But because I didn't pick up on what he seemed to have been thinking, I couldn't empower myself or him to get more of the professional help he needed.

The **be nice.** action plan provides the knowledge and confidence to take the necessary steps to help a person who is struggling with depression get the help he or she needs. It's a tool that provides the same kind of prevention that "stop, drop, and roll" does for a fire. When we think of someone caught in a fire, we know to give this most basic and urgent advice of stopping, dropping, and rolling.

When we think of someone stuck in depression, we hear silence. The acrostic **be nice.** is easy to understand and implement in a crisis situation. Not only does it improve lives, it can save lives too. **be nice.** has changed my life and the lives of many others. It is changing the way people think about and respond to mental illness, depression, and potential suicide.

The fact that one out of every four people in the world will suffer with some level of depression or mental illness this year, and that nearly one-half of those people will not seek or receive professional treatment, demands a large-scale response. Depression is a painful but unaddressed illness for those who have it; it's an invisible one for those who don't. That has to change.

That's where we all have an opportunity to help—to arm ourselves with the tools we need to address this illness and help those who are struggling with it. It begins with our loved ones but should extend to friends and acquaintances wherever we're engaged in our communities. That's where you come in. I didn't know how to help Wayne at the time. You have the opportunity to arm yourself with the tools that can help yourself and others.

After reading the be nice. book (the companion book to this book that teaches the *be nice.* program), I am convinced that you will be equipped as I am with the easiest action plan to help change, improve, and save lives from depression and suicide. My hope is that you will help me to carry out my brother Wayne's wishes as well as so many others who have succumbed to mental illness by suicide to help others overcome the illness of depression before it takes more lives.

Do You Need Immediate Help?

For Immediate help,
call the 988 Suicide and Crisis Lifeline,
available 24/7.
https://988lifeline.org/media-resources/
"If you or someone you know is experiencing a mental health or
substance use crisis, call or text 988"

Order your copy of *be nice. – 4 SIMPLE STEPS to Recognize Depression and Prevent Suicide* at www.benicebook.org or at Amazon.

All net proceeds for the sale of the be nice. book go to support the work of the Mental Health Foundation of West Michigan and the Wayne Elhart be nice. Memorial Fund.

How the be nice. Program Is Helping to Solve this Pervasive Problem—Changing the Culture with be nice.

Mental illness, particularly depression, is expected to be one of the major health burdens of the coming decades—affecting schools, businesses, and other organizations. Considering that depression is one of the main causes of chronic illness in the developed world, it stands to reason that we need to equip both children and adults to manage and treat it—to recognize it in themselves and others, and to know what steps to take to get help. This needs to be an open discussion that produces knowledge, then confidence, and then appropriate tools to take action.

This is where the be nice. action plan provides fuel for the race to educate our youth and adults about mental illness awareness and suicide prevention. The simplicity of the be nice. Action Plan makes it scaleable. It is easy to embrace. It is simple to engage a community like it has been embraced by the community of West Michigan and quickly growing into other parts of the U.S. and the world. It is creating a common language and a culture of connection, and it is saving lives.

Join the movement in your community with be nice.!

Here's how:

upstream prevention
through mental health education

be nice. equips individuals to recognize changes at the onset of an illness. This is an an upstream approach.

be nice. is a mental health and suicide prevention program that has an action plan. When used effectively, the **be nice.** program encourages individuals to challenge themselves and others to seek appropriate professional help when they notice changes in their mental health.

We are creating psychologically safe communities by:

- **EDUCATING** individuals of all ages to recognize the signs of mental illness and have the confidence to take action when helping themselves or others.

- **EDUCATING** communities to support the mental, emotional, and behavioral health of all individuals.

- **EDUCATING** individuals to reduce the shame, stigma, and secrecy surrounding mental illnesses and treatment so less people struggle silently and more people seek help.

- **EDUCATING** individuals about the warning signs of suicide and equipping them with the tools to act when someone is in crisis.

Visit: benice.org

be nice. deemed to be best practice.

Results from an evidenced-based study conducted with Grand Valley State University show:

- Increases mental health awareness and resources available among staff, students, and parents
- Decreases the number of behavioral referrals and bullying incidents
- Provides a common language to discuss negative behaviors
- Increase in suicide prevention behaviors
- Improves climate and connectedness while increasing positive behaviors
- Integrates well with other character and behavioral school-based programs
- Identified top-down support as most effective for successful implementation
- Sustainable with training and support provided by the Mental Health Foundation of West Michigan

a common language

education for all ages

confidence to take action when it comes to mental health

a sustainable program

community level awareness

Visit: benice.org

be nice. Programming

be nice. Business is a sustainable programming model utilizing business liaisons through a train-the-trainer method. A company's **be nice.** liaison will use the trainings and materials to bring the action plan to the work environment—helping to cultivate a psychologically safe work environment. For businesses of any size!

Visit: benicebusiness.org

be nice. Schools is an evidence-based, K-12 systematic approach to behavioral and mental health education and awareness. The **be nice.** program is a district-wide initiative to be implemented year after year. Repetition creates familiarity making the **be nice.** action plan common language. The goal is for students, school and support staff, and families to feel comfortable talking openly and honestly about mental health. It's proven that **be nice.** students are more apt to utilize resources if they are struggling or let a trusted adult know if they're worried about a friend. Once your school has successfully launched the first year of programming, **be nice.** chapters renew their membership each year to have continued access to new tools and supplies for sustaining the program.

Visit: beniceschools.org

be nice. Faith trains liaisons from faith communities to create movement for mental health throughout their congregation. The **be nice.** action plan is a tool for the larger community to increase positive understanding of mental health, as well as a tool in one-on-one conversations. For some, faith is the number one protective factor in mental health—make sure that your faith community is prepared with the tools to begin these conversations about mental health, and empower members with resources, hope, and understanding.

Visit: benicefaith.org

be nice. Community: Whether educating groups of organizations on the **be nice.** action plan for mental health and suicide prevention, or hosting stigma-reducing events, **be nice.** community helps to cultivate connectedness and ultimately improves, changes, and saves lives.

Visit: benice.org